The Guidebook to your

INNER POWER

By

Amelia Bert

ameliabert.com

TABLE OF CONTENTS

PART 1

BEGINNERS ON THE SPIRITUAL PATH 1

PART 2

ADVANCED SPIRITUALISTS............... 115

PART 3

SPIRITUAL MASTERS 177

PREFACE

When I was new in spirituality I was fascinated with all the information and experiences that I came across. All the things I thought were impossible, or that I only saw in movies I discovered them to be probable; telepathic communication, energy healing, past regression, communication with spirit and so much more. I was so intrigued; I wanted to learn everything I could about our inner power and all it can achieve. The paths lead me to create this book and share it with you.

I tried to find one book that contains several steps and guidance towards spiritual practices; I failed. I came across separate information online, or multiple books on different matters, but not one book that included them all. Several years later and after many practices, lessons, failed attempts and great determination, I collected all the information I needed and I present them all in this book.

If you follow my work as a spiritual author and a spiritual counselor, you will know that I have achieved spirit communication and I work closely with lighted beings such as Angels with all my projects, including this book. The information provided is a combination of Divine narration, personal experiences, as well as recollection of others' successful attempts and processes. No matter if you are new or advanced in the spiritual path, you will find valuable information and tips to help you with several practices. This book is for all of you that want to know all they can about spirituality and their inner power.

All the techniques and practices are carefully chosen and studied and there are successful testimonies of people who were fruitful using them. Rest assured that anything that is presented can be achieved, and you have the power to do it.

I hope my teachings, lessons and guidance will help you find new ways to embrace your inner power, and expand your wisdom. Do not let anyone tell you it is impossible as this book is a proof that everything can be achieved if you believe. May this guide be a doorway to your very own inner super-powers.

INTRODUCTION

All the topics provided are based on spiritual processes that expand the spirit. Being spiritual as a term means developing or connecting to that part of you that is spirit. Spirit is our essence, our soul, our inner world. When we return to the non-physical all that we are left with, is the spirit. When we come back and reincarnate in the physical world, we keep all the lessons and skills of our soul. As we enter in a physical body all skills and memories are hidden, but they are all there. As we work with our spirit we can remember them, work with them, and practice them. Spiritual practices work with that inner part of us that still holds great knowledge from many other worlds.

Any skills that we may have had in any other lifetime, and even techniques we use as a spirit, we have them locked up within. This book does not try to teach you anything new, but helps you to remember what you already have locked within. Everyone can succeed in the methods since we are all special, we all have a soul, we all have knowledge that is connected with the cosmos. All you have to do is believe and practice.

There are all those physical processes and tasks that one can develop working with their body such as running, dancing, skiing. On the other hand, there are those practices that have little to do with working with your body, but practice alignment with the mind. Those require thought, such as mathematics, problem solving and so forth. A third kind of practice does not require neither body nor the mind, but the spirit. It focuses on creativity, inspiration, belief and energy. As you are about to discover, spiritual practices exclude any kind of thought and even physical activity in order to embrace the spirit and its knowledge.

Practice is necessary for any task to help you get better. This is true for spiritual practices as well. As you work with your spirit, you gradually learn to let go of your bodily functions, such as movement and thought, and embrace your spiritual ones. While in spirit you don't need to use your feet to walk but you teleport, you don't use your tongue to talk but you use telepathy, you don't think, because you know so much already. Similarly, as you practice spiritual processes you must let go of the body and mind temporarily, in order to embrace the powers of the spirit, similar to when you were only nonphysical. We can use our body and enjoy material pleasures, the mind that helps us make decisions based on our free will and we have the soul that is our essence and is so very wise. Nonetheless, we are used to the body and mind and we have excluded the spirit from our everyday activities. As we work with our spirit, we gain skills, unconditional wisdom, guidance and inner happiness. The more you work with your spirit, the wiser and happier you become. Sadness and depression comes from the mind that holds the ego that is a physical resonance. Spirits, Angels and anyone that doesn't have a physical body, are pure and happy. The more you embrace your spiritual side, the more blissful and carefree you become.

This book gives you the steps to succeed in each process, as well as offers you explanations to help you understand the power within each method. It is divided in three parts starting from the easiest and most necessary in the section called "Beginners", moving to "advanced" and finally to the chapter "master techniques" that focuses on more detailed and complex processes and techniques.

The steps are easy to follow and include several approaches to help you find the ones that work for you. There may be many other explanations, details and approaches for each technique however I chose the most important and helpful ones to help you get started. If you want a more thorough explanation or more advanced methods and techniques, please do expand your knowledge with more books or courses that focus on the specific domain of your interest.

To conclude this introduction, I recommend you to try the processes with an open mind to get the best results. Feel free to use them as you please but be aware of the law of karma. "Do not do to others what you do not want done to yourself." Use the practices for knowledge and expansion and with only goodness and love at heart. This is the way to succeed, and unlock further spiritual gifts. You have the power already within.

PART 1

BEGINNERS ON THE SPIRITUAL PATH

1. HOW TO MEDITATE

This chapter goes first in this guide because it is one of the most important routines of a spiritualist. It is essential to allow some time in your daily schedule for meditation. It helps in many ways both spiritually and physically. It expands and progress you, calms, soothes you, and helps you connect with your Divine self. The more in alignment you are with your higher self, the more you progress spiritually.

Some of the benefits of meditation are: relaxation, serenity and peace, enhancing spiritual connection, empowering intuition, receiving guidance from your spirit guides and Angels, connecting with a loved one, feelings of euphoria and love, growth of spiritual gifts, alignment of mind and body, empowerment.

Every time you meditate, you unravel more of its benefits. The great thing about meditation is that it is never the same. This may sound strange if you are a beginner at meditating, since the thought is always the same: quiet your mind; however it is so much more. It becomes a journey, an expansion of self.

When I was a beginner in meditation, I only had one goal: do not fall asleep. I have to be honest, there were times that I did fall asleep; but I insisted. I allowed twenty minutes daily and it took me about a month to discover how amazing meditation really is. After the first month, not only I didn't fall asleep anymore, but I discovered that every time I was taken in higher realms. With meditation, you let go of my body but your soul is on a journey, every time the journey is different. Sometimes, I feel the pure strong emotions of love and peace, other times I interact with loving spirits. There were times I saw Mother Mary herself. One time, I even visited a past life, and in another I connected with a future timeline holding my future child! The possibilities are endless and the power of a meditation is much more than just quieting your mind.

Through meditation you can access the Akashic records of all knowledge, see and talk to you spirit guides, connect with a lost loved one, work with the Angels, and even go into past lives. To be able to channel spirit successfully, meditation is the key.

Determination is a significant strength for meditation; if you can succeed in meditating every day, after the first month you won't do without it. The good news is, even if you find it hard at first, it always gets easier. It doesn't matter if you fall asleep sometimes, keep going and you will be greatly rewarded.

If you are ready to begin, I present the steps that help me meditate successfully.

STEPS TO MEDITATE

1. Clear your schedule for twenty minutes or more. Find a comfortable place that you will not get disrupted.

2. Light a candle and burn some essential oils, and if you prefer have some appropriate crystals nearby. (Find a guide to crystals on chapter 15, and the guide for essential oils on 2) This step is not necessary, but it will help you relax. Set your timer to the necessary length, so that you can easily bring back your conscious.

3. Be in a comfortable sitting position and play some meditation music. I found that headphones work best to eliminate any external sounds. At this point, you should decide if you want a guided meditation or simply music. A guided meditation is spoken word along with soothing music that guides your imagery and helps you achieve a goal. I have created a set of guided meditation that I created with the Angels. You can find them here: bit.ly/24qLSRq

If you simply want some soothing you can use my own playlist from YouTube. http://bit.ly/26wxjgc

4. Set an intention in your mind. What do you want to achieve with this meditation? Relaxation? Connect with your guides? Enhance your intuition? Then invite the Angels to surround you.

> *"I call upon the most lighted Angels and spirit guides that can most assist me please join me in this meditation and help me to _____. Also shield and protect me, and be with me until this meditation is complete. Thank you, and so it is."*

5. Close your eyes and just listen. Remove any thoughts, if they come, let them go and continue focusing on the music. Listen to all the sounds, notice the notes that you hear, and allow your mind to relax. You can also try some of the following techniques to help you with this step.

a. Count your breaths and focus on how your stomach moves.

b. Hum the note "Mm" in your mind as in this way your mind will be occupied with thought and you won't allow any other thoughts to join you, nor fall asleep.

c. Choose a music you like and focus on one instrument or sound.

d. Visualize white starting from the bottom of your feet and rising up. Every part that the light touches removes tension and relaxes it completely. Start slowly and finish at the top of your crown.

e. Visualize a stairwell going downwards. Each step you take you will feel yourself more and more relaxed. When you reach the final step your whole body is completely tension free.

6. I find that the first ten minutes are necessary to remove my thoughts. After that, I am calmer and I feel my body let go of any tension. If this step is successful, your body will become heavy and you will need effort to move. That is a very good sign of a relaxed body. Now allow the Angels to guide you whatever you need to go, and enjoy the journey.

7. When the timer sets, or the music finishes, stay still for a few seconds to regain your consciousness. Do not try to stand immediately, but allow some time to ground back to your physical body.

8. Write down any experiences on your diary. It always helps to try and understand what you have experienced.

9. Ground yourself. If you have experienced deep meditation state, you might feel dizzy, lightheaded, or with a headache. That is normal, all you have to do is some grounding to fully connect to your physical body. See chapter 7 on how to techniques.

- If you are at a beginner level, try twenty minutes of meditation, and you can add to it whenever you feel you can handle more minutes. I started with twenty and went up to forty minutes and even to an hour. I know this is not convenient for many, and it is okay; it is not necessary how many minutes you allow, but the frequency. Try to meditate at least five days a week.

- Some people may find it extremely difficult to meditate. There I suggest some guided meditations. If that doesn't work, try some adult coloring. It does not have the same effect, but it helps to quiet the mind and deepen the bond with one's higher self.

- Meditate with crystals. Some crystals and gemstones have a light energy that help you relax and achieve deep meditation. For detailed instruction on handling crystals and gems see chapter 3.

  a. Cleanse your crystals.

  b. Choose a crystal with the qualities that can help you in meditation. I suggest clear or rose quartz or amethyst.

  c. Place the crystal near you or hold it in your hand. I find that placing a stone on my third eye helps me absorb its energy much faster.

2. HOW TO USE ESSENTIAL OILS

Essential oil is a liquid that is extracted from various plants and flowers. Each one has a different aroma which contains different qualities that passes on to the person who uses it.

Essential oils are natural products that come from nature, and like anything that comes from Mother Nature, consists of special high energy. They have been used for thousands of years in medicine, cosmetics and for spiritual empowerment.

In this chapter I enlist some of the spiritual benefits of essential oils. Bare in mind, there are different qualities with any oil you use, but the most common benefits include relaxation, grounding, spiritual connection, happiness, peace, purification, relieving stress, inspiration, creativity, and cleansing.

Ways to use

1. **Inhaling.** There a few ways to do this method.

a. My favorite one is using a candle warmer. You can find such item in stores and online. Fill the candle warmer with water, and add two drops of your favorite essential oil. Place the candle below and light it. As that water boils, the essential oil appears in the fumes and fills the air. Remember to be near the candle warmer if you are in a big room.

b. Use a diffuser. Add a few drops of the oil in the diffuser, and allow it to evaporate, and fill the room with its powerful smell.

c. Purchase ready sticks with your favorite essential oil. Let the stick burn and enjoy the effects.

d. If you don't have a candle warmer, or an essential oil stick, you might as well add a drop of the liquid on a cotton tissue. You will be able smell the essential oil and get its effects.

e. Steam it. Boil water with a few drops of the essential oil, and the fumes will fill the room.

f. Spray. Create your favorite essential oil mix with a lot of water into a spray bottle. Spray on your hands and in the room to get its effect.

2. Massage oil. Don't add the liquid directly on the body, but add a few drops with your massage oil. There are also ready to use massage oils with essential oils.

3. Bath. Add a few drops inside your filled water bath tub and enjoy the relaxation.

4. Consume. Some people add a few drops in their water, however I don't recommend it. There is not yet a research that confirms if there are any risks with consuming essential oils. Until this is done, I don't advice it.

So now that you know how to use them I have done my research and I bring you a list with the most popular essential oils and their usages.

The qualities of each essential oil might not be similar to everyone. They have different effects according to one's energy and personality. Essential oils are unique, and so are your bodies and attributes.

Feel free to use this guide and choose your own favorites.

ESSENTIAL OILS AND THEIR ATTRIBUTES:

Allspice – Ease, nurture, comfort

Amyris – Centering, relaxation, removes anxiety, eases muscle tension

Anise – euphoric, calming, sedative

Basil – Clarity, raising energy, upliftment, relaxation

Bergamont – inspiration, upliftment, stress- reliever, confidence

Cardamom seed – comfort, relief, seductive

Cassia – energizing, comfort, seductive

Cedarwood – spiritual power, ease, comfort, empowerment

Chamomile – calming, relaxing, soothing, warming

Cinnamon – stress-reliever

Clary Sage – center, balance, euphoric

Clove – comfort

Coriander – nurturing, aphrodisiac

Cypress – balance, center, energy

Eucalyptus – cleansing, purification

Fennel – Restoring, soothing, energy flow

Frankincense – calming, sedative, relaxing

Geranium – Balance, raise of energy and mood, calming

Ginger – Centering, strengthening, balancing, grounding

Grapefruit – cleansing, refreshing, elevating

Jasmine – relaxing, peaceful, alluring

Juniper Berry – cleansing, restoring, centering

Lavender – soothing, meditative, spiritual connection

Lemon – energizing, elevating

Lime – clearing, energizing

Marjoram – balancing, soothing

Myrrh – cleansing, centering, meditative

Orange – purifying, balancing, uplifting

Oregano – cleansing, uplifting

Patchouli – soothing, grounding, ease, romantic

Peppermint – energizing, cleansing

Rose – raising vibration, nurturing, balancing

Rosemary – Clarity

Sandalwood – grounding, relaxing

Spearmint – vitalizing

Tangerine – uplifting, cleansing

Tea Tree – cleansing, purifying, stabilizing

Thyme – cleansing, energizing

Vanilla – soothing, balancing

Vetiver – Grounding

Wintergeen – soothing, refreshing

Ylang – Ylang - meditative, euphoric, purifying, spiritual connection

3. HOW TO USE CRYSTALS AND GEMSTONES

Crystals and gemstones come from earth. It is a pure element that holds high energy, and special spiritual powers. Working with crystals, or even having them around the house can be a powerful ally to enhance your spiritual techniques. There are books specifically discussing the abilities of crystals and gems, as well as a lot of courses on how to work with them. In this guide I give you the basic information you need to get started, as well as a list with the most common crystals and gems that you should consider adding in your collection.

The list of the benefits of crystals and gems are just as vast as their variety. Some of their benefits include: spiritual empowerment, protection, purification, high vibration, clearer connection with spirit, healing. All those qualities are passed on to the person who wears them, uses them, or is near them.

When buying a crystal you should spent some time observing it, holding it and sensing its energy. It is vital that you feel drawn to the crystal before you buy it. This way you ensure that your energies match and confirm that the crystal's powers will benefit you the most. Follow your intuition and discover which crystal or gem gets your attention. It might be a feeling, a knowing, the crystal or gem might feel cold or very warm in your hands. Consider the following questions: Does it feel good in your hand? How do you feel near it? What emotions does it bring up when you hold it?

Furthermore, it is believed that a crystal or gemstone chooses you. If you find it online, or it was a gift to you, then it most definitely found you and your energies align.

Crystals and gems are not typical rocks. If they are mishandled, or they are in a negative environment they get damaged. This is common for crystals or gemstones that absorb negative energy. If they are not cleansed from that energy, it harms them. They might receive cracks, lose their shine, change their color, or even break. Have an eye out for those cracks when you purchase a crystal or gem, or prefer the ones that were not cut. For the market today, they tend to cut bigger stones in smaller pieces just to sell them faster. The split gets imprinted in the stone and results in weakness of their qualities.

Crystals and gemstones also have reflexes and they can even move. I have heard many stories from owners who place them in another room and find them in another.

Ways to benefit from the power of crystal or gemstone

1. Wear them. Since they hold power, having them that close to you transfer a boost of their power onto you. Whether their power is protection or spiritual enhancement, it is always a good idea to have one with you.

2. Have crystals near you. If you can't wear them, have them in your wallet, near your pillow at night, or on the desk where you work. They can project their benefits in their close environment.

3. Hold them as you meditate, or as you channel spirit. Some crystals help to boost your spiritual connection.

4. Clean your chakras. See chapter 34 on ways to clean chakras.

5. Place some crystals on corners of your house or room for safety. Create a square grid or pyramid with your crystals or gems. They protect and cleanse the center of that square or pyramid. Better stones offer better protection for spaces.

6. Healing. There are techniques that you can work with these powerful stones to help someone heal from emotional or physical illness. Study the technique, or hire a crystal healer to help you out.

7. Have a stone under your pillow at night. Some stones help to improve sleep, help you remember dreams or connect you with the Divine through dreams.

8. **Pendulum dowsing:** your crystals can be used to answer questions, and receive guidance from the Ether. See chapter 28 on how to use pendulum dowsing.

There are plenty more ways to use Crystals. If you are interested consider purchasing a book solely on Crystals and their usage.

Ways to cleanse your crystal or gemstone

Since these stones are very sensitive, they capture negative energies from their environment. Before you work with them, make sure you cleanse them so they work properly, and that they do not pass on to you any of the captured low energy. When you cleanse a stone, you return it to their natural high frequency state, it needs to benefit you.

There are a lot of ways that help you stone get purified. Here I only name a few.

1. **Wash them in a river, sea, or lake.** Nature washes away their negative energy and restores them.

2. **Burry them in the soil overnight**. This will restore them to their natural state.

3. **Sage**: You have heard of this before, your grandmother was doing, in the movies they are doing it, well, it's time you do this as well. Smudging eliminates any negative entities, energies and intentions. This is a powerful cleansing method. I suggest you have a sage bundle handy. Buy a sage smudge stick, a dried white sage or a white ceremonial sage bundle. You will find them in local herb shop or health store, metaphysical store, or my favorite: online shops.

a. For your sage clearing first, hold the sage and move it around your body. Visualize any negative energy lifting off your body, out of your home, and into oblivion.

b. Place it in safe bowl and get ready to burn it. As the sage burns, it emits powerful clearing smoke. Go around with the house passing on the smoke in all rooms and places you want to clear, including people. Hold the intention that the sage will extinguish any negativity and purify any energy that is close.

4. **Omm**. Hum that sound as you hold your stone and that will cleanse it. As you do, have the intention that any negative energy is cleared away.

5. **Invocation and visualization**. Hold the crystal and focus your attention on it being cleansed. Visualize a white lighted energy, and feel purification and love entering the stone.

"We call upon the Divine energies of Angels; ask that they become a part of this crystal. Cleanse it, clear it, and purify it. Thank you for your assistance, and so it is."

6. **Sunlight**. Leave the stones in direct sunlight for a few hours. It will rejuvenate them.

7. **Salt water**. Similar to bathing in the ocean, salt absorbs negative energies. You should fill a glass or metal bowl and place your stones in in a way that they are fully covered in the salt water. Leave them between 1 to 24 hours, depending on how big they are. Then rinse them with clear running water.

Caution: *Not all stones can be added in salt as they can be damaged. Such stones are Pyrite, Lapis Lazuli, Opal, Hematite.*

8. **Crystal singing bowl.** There is a special bowl that omits high vibrational sounds that help to cleanse your crystals. For more information go to chapter 11.

9. **Full moon**. Similar to the sunlight, the full moon recharges and restores them. Leave them somewhere safely outside on a night with a full moon.

How to reprogram your crystals:

Crystals need to be assigned their roles. When they recognize their purpose, they will live up to it in order to please you. You want to know your soul path, so you can fulfill it, similarly, stones work to fulfill the path you assign to them. Have a look at their qualities before you assign them a purpose, as it is better to combine their qualities with their purpose in order to be able to fulfill it.

Intention is what you need to program them.

1. Firstly, cleanse your stone as described above.

2. Then, hold your crystal in you left hand and think of what you want it to help you with. For better results, speak to is as well and assign it a purpose verbally.

You can give also give a stone more than one purpose.

- The bigger the stone, the more power it holds.

- You need to cleanse your crystals regularly, especially before healing, or after they have been exposed to negative energies such as a fight.

- Crystals get damaged or warn out with negative energy. If you notice your crystal gains cracks it is a sign it is weak.

- Be careful when purchasing crystals or gems, and notice their pattern. Many stones are broken into smaller pieces to sell separately and you can easily notice the damage. Such stones may be weaker and hold negative energy, so be careful before you buy.

- You can also talk to your crystals. Yes this is very common if you have a clair ability. Hold your crystal or gemstone and ask it a question. The answers of the crystal will come either as thoughts in your mind (clairaudient ability) or as mental images (clairvoyant ability). This can be very useful as you can tune into your crystal and ask them how they can most serve you. Don't worry if you don't have a clair ability developed yet, there are a few chapters in this book to help you. (44, 45

CRYSTALS, GEMSTONES AND THEIR QUALITIES

Amethyst: Develops intuition, 3rd eye awakening, helps in meditation.

Ametrine: cleansing, energizing, boosting

Agate: enhances strength, confidence, healing

Amazonite: brings inspiration, self-confidence, truth, grounding

Aquamarine: tranquility, peace, protection

Aventurine: brings inner calmness, inspiration, balance, healing

Apophyllite: meditation, spiritual connection

Apatite: peace, focus, grounding

Bloodstone: Self-esteem, strength, healing, creativity

Black Tourmaline: cleansing, protection, grounding, strength

Blue lace agate: courage, truth, peace, empowerment

Carnelian: confidence, motivation, karma balancing

Chysoprase: receptiveness, kindness, compassion

Citrine: abundance, prosperity, self-esteem, happiness

Clear quartz: Clarity, empowerment, energy, focus, healing

Coral: Harmony, energy, joy, creativity

Emerald: love, harmony

Fluorite: memory, concentration, order, relaxation

Fuchsite: intuition, self-clarity, self-growth

Garnet: healing, energy, flow

Hematite: protection, grounding, protection, courage, balance

Howlite: calmness, peace

Jade: focus, inspiration, will, wealth, wisdom, peace

Jasper: control, tranquility, healing, self-control

Labratorite: protection, aura cleansing, wisdom

Lapis Lazuli: Enlightenment, protection, spiritual connection, awareness, clarity

Muscovite: centering, remove blockages, awakening, spiritual connection

Malachite: insight, strength, transformation, confidence

Moonstone: wisdom, nurture, harmony, protection, fertility

Onyx: protection, against negative attacks, healing

Serpentine: love, meditation, peace

Pyrite: protection, grounding, abundance, confidence, wealth

Phodonite: generosity, love, inspiration, well-being

Rhodotochrosite: empowerment, self-love, power, peace, joy

Peridot: insight, abundance, balance, harmony, beauty

Pink tourmaline: happiness, enthusiasm, energy

Rose quartz: love, calmness, inspiration, inner peace

Ritulated quartz: guidance, healing, empowerment, growth

Sodalite: clarity, joy, awakens third eye, brings intuition and insight

Selenite: awareness, telepathy, clarity

Smokey quartz: grounding, focus, connects to earth

Tiger's eye: stability, wealth, integrity, fortune success, bravery

Tourmalinated quartz: balance, wealth, stability

Turquoise:health, communication, peace, luck

Fascinated with the powers of crystals and gemstones I began to collect them, care, polish, recharge and energize them and add them in a crystal shop on the website: ameliabert.com to get your own share of pure energy.

4. HOW TO SHIELD/ For protection

Whether you are an empath, or you practice communication with spirit, you should shield regularly as energies, thoughts and intentions tend to affect everyone.

Empathic people are affected by multiple energies in a bigger level since, like crystals; they absorb energy from their environment. Everyone is an empath at a certain level since we all transmit and receive energy and we get affected by our environment. Shielding protects you from any external energy that may lower your own.

The following methods are for protection against negative thoughts such as jealousy or meaning to do harm that is directed to you, to those close to you, or even to your home.. Also, shielding protects against absorbing another's low energies and negative emotions, it helps against spirits of lower energy that may be present in a room, or that may prevent your channeling or readings. Shielding before meditation also prevents low energy spirits from getting in tune with you.

Additionally, shielding empowers our positive thoughts and removes any negative ones from our state of mind. The good news is that that shielding is so easy to do, but repetition is needed as the protection fades. I would suggest twice a day for Empaths, and once a day for the rest; or also, use whenever you feel the need.

Also, I recommend shielding before attempting any divination techniques or communication with spirit.

Ways for protection:

1. **White light protection:** Close your eyes and with your intention or words, invite white light to join you for protection. With your mind's eye then, imagine white light surrounding your body. Your intention does the rest.

2. **Invoking Angel protection.** Who is better for shielding than Archangel Michael?

> *Silently pray: "Archangel Michael of the light, I call upon you to embrace me with your Divine Light and shield me against any negative energies, negative thoughts, negative spirits and negative people. Thank you, and so it is."*

For this prayer, make sure that you apprehend each word as your attention is required for the Archangel Michael to understand what you need. Remember, spirits know energy and attention, not words.

3. **Your energy is your greatest or worst ally.** If you achieve high energy then you create a very powerful tool for protection.

As you are positive and you have high energy, you are surrounded by people, events and energies that match that positive frequency. In the instances that you are in sync with your own divinity, the energy that flows through you is so powerful that no lower energy can touch nor affect you.

When your own energy is raised, your own intention is more than enough to be protected. For ways to raise your vibration, read next chapter.

4. **Wear a special Stone.** Crystals or gemstones come from earth, for this they hold special energy. Wearing a special crystal locket will help to protect you against low energy attacks. There are various stones known for protection, such as the black tourmaline, amber, quartz, amethyst and many more. As stones are unique, they can be assigned the role of protection, even if they are not any of those mentioned above.

Reference to chapter 3 for working with Crystals and Gemstones.

5. **Call Spirit guides for protection.** Your spiritual team is there to help you out. Assign them to shield you continuously against any psychic attacks or low energies. They will know what to do.

- Being shielded or protected leaves out certain energies but also may prevent some good ones from joining you. Perhaps certain spirit guides that want to join your spiritual team cannot tune into you because your shielding blocks them. also, for healers, you maybe blocking out healing energy from making you its carrier in order to pass on energy healing to others. For this I suggest you are clear of what kind of shielding you wish to have before you create it. For instance the protective invocation in point 2 entails protection against negative energies, negative thoughts, negative spirits and against negative people.

- You can ask to take down your protective shield (a thought is enough) as it will shield your energy and not allow external energies to connect. This is especially true if you want to do a healing, or if you feel it interferes with your spiritual connection.

5. HOW TO RAISE YOUR VIBRATION AND CHARGE YOUR ENERGY

Raising your vibration entails a shift in your mood, positive energies and emotions. There is great power in an elevated mood as it is associated with inner power, peace and divinity.

There is a difference in being happy for a few moments, and from radiating inner bliss.

In the steps that follow I guide you to alter your vibration to benefit your whole being and not temporarily your mood. Paying attention to how you feel is the key, as it ensures that your energy and thus inner peace and power, are transformed into Divine peace and enlightenment. When your energy is raised more regularly than not, you are in sync with your own higher self, you are able to follow your intuition, find your life's path, communicate with lighted beings more clearly, and transform your life towards your greatest desires.

If I have convinced you of the benefits of raising your vibration, let's break down the ways you go about it.

WAYS TO RAISE YOUR VIBRATION:

You may try some of these, just one, or even create your own. Every one's energy and personality is different, so the processes that follow are only limited to help you get started.

1. **Absorb nature's pure energy:** Don't worry, nature has enough to give around. When you spent time in nature, your energy gets charged, and so your own vibration raises.

> **a**. Stand or sit under a tree. Close your eyes and feel the great energy of this powerful tree. Touch it with the intention to charge your own energy. You may even ask for the tree to lend you some of its energy.

> **b.** Swim in the ocean

> **c**. Walk barefoot on the ground, or on the sand.

> **d**. Gardening. You spent time within flowers and plants that help you uplifit your mood.

2. **Spent time with animals.** Animals have their own energy, they live according to their own rules and they like it. There are even several psychological experiments with playing in a room full of kittens. They found that is highly stressed relieving. Play with your dog or cat, feed your rabbit, talk to your bird. They raise your vibration and help you unload and have a good time.

3. Be around babies and children. The same as with animals, young people are more in alignment with their divinity and their spirit, for this their energy is elevated regularly. When you spent time around them, your own energy gets a piece of their mood. Of course don't scold them, but play with them, be a kid once again.

4. Talk to positive people. Some have achieved inner bliss and quiet. for this, they have high vibration that even being near them helps you relax and have fun. Just by talking to them, your own energy will raise.

5. This may be obvious but: **Do what you love to do.** It may be a hobby, it may be an activity, it may be talking to a person. Whenever you feel the need for a break or an elevation, engage with it.

6. Work with Crystals. Like I have already mentioned in the chapter with Crystals, they hold special energy, because they come from Mother Nature. Simply holding a crystal or wearing a crystal locket, will help you to raise your vibrations. Crystals that will help you with that are: Moldovite, Kyanite, Black obsidian.

There is a whole chapter in this book on how to work with crystals. Reference chapter 3.

7. Smile. Of course you knew that. Smiling sends signals to the brain that you are happy and so it begins to loosen your nerves and relax you.

8. Eat healthy. I am obviously not a dietician and I know you are sick of hearing this, but coming out of a spiritualist perspective, eating green food, fruits, and plenty of water is consuming Nature's energy into your body and thus, raising your vibrations.

9. **Meditate**. The ultimate tip for spiritualists. When you meditate you release thought. In your thoughts there are any negative emotions. In the process of releasing any such thoughts, your spirit is free and connected to your divinity, where love and happiness is a dominant feeling.

Reference to chapter 1 on how to meditate.

10. **Spent some time coloring or painting**. Similar to meditation, when you color or create an artwork, you are distracted, you release any thought, because you concentrate on the work of art in front of you. When the troubling thoughts, fear and stress vanish, beautiful emotions rise up. Needless to say, when the project is completed you feel more elevation and accomplishment.

I will soon release an adult coloring book that brings extra positive energy. Subscribe here to take the email: http://ameliabert.com/

11. **Move your body**. You are energy, your bodies are energy and when you move, you help that energy flow. When that energy flows, you feel better, elevated, your mood raises, thus your energy does as well. Try yoga, walking, exercising, and dancing. We are born to move, so let's try it more often!

12. **Be grateful.** When you think of the things you do have, you feel gratitude. Gratitude is a high energy emotion close to unconditional love. This feeling alone helps you raise your energy so high that you won't remember why you were angry a few hours ago.

Here I would suggest keeping a gratitude diary. It will remind you to return to that feeling often. The more frequently you bring up this emotion, the more powerful your spirit becomes. It is worthwhile spending a few minutes every day to fill your diary.

13. **Breathe in patterns.** As we get absorbed in our everyday lives, we forget to breath. We only absorb half of the oxygen we should. Oxygen equals nature, equals high energy. A good way to make sure you breathe in as oxygen as you should is to pay attention to your breathing. Breath in, push the air down to your belly, wait for three seconds and then breathe out slowly. Whenever you are in need for some raised energy, repeat this breathing exercise and count to twenty.

A great pattern is: breathe in, pause for 1-2 seconds, release, and pause for 1-2 seconds repeat.

Another one is: breathe in deeply, pause for 5 seconds, release slowly counting to 5 and repeat.

14. **Enjoy the moment.** All you live is the present moment. There are so many things happening at once that you have to pause regularly to observe. Step back for a few seconds regularly and just observe, notice, enjoy. There is so much beauty in the present moment and so much energy that may otherwise slip through your fingers. Stop and notice so you can relax and raise your own energy in the process.

15. **Aromatherapy.** Essential oils, have a lot of benefits, one of them is raising your vibration. Light a candle and let that essential oil burn. As you absorb the natural scent, your vibrations will rise and you will relax enough to let go of any troubles. For the purpose of raising energy the following essential oils work best: Lavender, Bergamot, Geranium, Lemon, Basil, Orange, Rosewood, Jasmine, Ylang Ylang.

For a guide on essential oils go to chapter 2.

16. **Channeling lighted beings.** Whenever the mood I am, every time I talk to my inner guidance, my spirit guides or the Angels, I always feel so much better. Ask the Angels to elevate your energy, they always come for help.

17. **Recognize beauty.** Whenever you appreciate something, you cannot feel a negative emotion. I dare you to look around right now and find ten things you like. Notice their pattern, colors, beauty. Appreciation ensures raised energy.

18. **Compliment yourself.** We all love compliments, they raise our confidence and help our energy levels rise. But why do you sit around and wait for anyone to give you a compliment? Stand in front of a mirror and begin complimenting yourself. You have so many great attributes and your opinion is the one that counts the most.

19. **Visualize your desires.** Desires make us happy. Happiness elevates our energy levels. Close your eyes and imagine all those things you want as if you have them now. Take as much time as you need to feel good, and remember, nothing is unachievable, if you see it with your mind's eye, you will soon bring it to life.

20. **Take a nap.** If you feel drained or low in energy, sometimes it is better to not do anything at all. Before you begin your nap state:

> *"I am going to have a wonderful nap, and when I wake up, my vibration will have been raised and I will rejuvenated and happy. And so it is."*

21. **Sunbathe.** The sun is full of energy. The plants need it to grow, we need it to be elevated. Just a few minutes under the sunlight will help you be rejuvenated.

6. HOW TO CLEANSE YOUR ENERGY AND THE ENERGY OF YOUR HOME

Sometimes, you try to raise your vibrations, but nothing is working. There are times you get confused and feel totally out of focus disoriented, drained and filled with thoughts. You may feel "stuck" in life. This means it is time to step away, and cleanse your energy.

To raise the existing energy, you must clear it first. Cleansing your energy is cleaning it from any negative frequencies, spirits, and chatter so you can find clarity and ease.

Your space gets affected by energies, as well. Objects contain energy and even rooms adjust to the energy of those around. When a room or house contains a lot of energy, it drains you when you are in it.

As you cannot cleanse your space without getting some clearing as well, I have included techniques for both clearing your energy as well as your house's.

WAYS OF CLEANSING ENERGY:

1. **Bath in the ocean.** The sea water contains natural salt that helps to clear our existing vibration. If you have the ocean close by, and it is not freezing cold, consider taking a swim regularly. You will feel rejuvenated and more relaxed. Those gray negative energies that lay in your aura will dissolve with the help of the salt.

2. **Have a salt bath.** If you don't have the ocean close by, this is the best alternative for obvious reasons. Fill that bath tub with water, as warm as you need, and add three handfuls of natural salt (sea salt or Himalayan crystal salt). Adding an essential oil such as peppermint and lighting candles will only make the clearing process more powerful. Sink in the water, relax and hold the intention of releasing all negative energy from your mind and body. Enjoy the relaxation for 15 minutes or more.

3. **Sage.** You have heard of this before, your grandmother was doing, in the movies they are doing it, well, it's time you do this as well. Smudging eliminates any negative entities, energies and intentions. This is a powerful cleansing method. I suggest you have a sage bundle handy. Buy a sage smudge stick, a dried white sage or a white ceremonial sage bundle. You will find them in local herb shop or health store, metaphysical store, or my favorite: online shops.

> **a.** For your sage clearing first, hold the sage and move it around your body. Visualize any negative energy lifting off your body, out of your home, and into oblivion.

> **b.** Place it in safe bowl and get ready to burn it. As the sage burns, it emits powerful clearing smoke. Go around with the house passing on the smoke in all rooms and places you want to clear, including people. Hold the intention that the sage will extinguish any negativity and purify any energy that is close.

4. Aromatherapy. Some essential oils hold purification energy, which helps to clear away negativity. Let those essential oils burn with the help of a candle and the fumes will help to clear your energy, the room that they are in, as well as those around you. Since this handbook is to help you make the most out of everything, I list all essential oils that you can use to clear your energy: Rose, peppermint, frankincense, lavender, basil, cypress, juniper, Myrrh, sage, Palo santo, Cedarwood, sandalwood, cinnamon, rosemary, eucalyptus.

For a guide on Essential oils, go to chapter 2.

5. De-clutter your space. All those furniture, objects, machines and anything else that is in your home, contain energy. A space full of things lying around expands the room's existing energy and that creates a chaotic sensation to those who live in it.

Even Angels and spirits don't like a chaotic room, it interferes with their energy. Before you try to connect with an Angel or spirit, make sure that tidy around the room first.

Get rid of anything that you don't use, donate those old toys, re-freshen the flowers in the vase, do laundry, open the windows to let fresh air in, and tidy the house. This will help you feel like a weight has lifter and you will gain clarity.

There is more on this subject read how to use feng sui 9.

6. Chant "Om". I know, I was skeptical of this at first, but since I have tried it, there is absolutely no doubt of how powerful this mantra is.

This sound is not just syllables pronounced together, but frequency that holds extensive energy. If repeated, it welcomes that energy into your environment that purifies your thoughts and aura. It is clearing, relaxing and powerful. It has been used through many centuries, especially in Buddhism, the more it has been used, the more power it holds.

Chant this Omm sound within or out loud, as often as you need.

   a. In a quiet place close your eyes with the intention of centering and clearing your being. b. Close your eyes and chant the sound. Notice how your frequency changes with every repeat.

   b. Let go and welcome the clearing of your chakras.

To cleanse your home with this method, chant out loud or simply find the audio of this mantra and turn up the volume. Open the windows to free any negative energy that releases as the sound reaches the syllable m.

Here is a link to an Om chanting:

https://www.youtube.com/watch?v=HLhld_L1WBA

7. Visualize white light. As you have learned by now, intention is your most powerful ally. Close your eyes and imagine a white energy surrounding your body, or house. Direct this energy:

   "Please protect me and my home from any negative intention, energies, and spirits and remove them completely."

White light is a very powerful form of Divine assistance. With minimal attention, you create a protective shield and clear away energy.

I suggest you combine this method along with the next one.

8. Angel detox. Angels are always there to help. With intention you invoke them, with a prayer you allow them to help you.

"Angels of the light that can most assist me now, please join me and help to cleanse and uplift my energy, as well as the energy of this room; release any form of negativity into the light. This is for the greatest and highest good, thank you, and so it is."

9. Crystal cleansing. There are certain crystals that purify the energy of those who use them. Crystals are also used in energy healing to clearing the chakras and activate Divine energy within. Wearing a crystal locket will help your energy stay cleansed. Having these certain crystals around your home, will also absorb any negative energies.

Such crystals are: Black tourmaline, Smokey quartz, Rose Quartz, amethyst. There is a complete list of crystals and their qualities in chapter 3.

10. Consuming blessed water. Water can be assigned properties before it is consumed. It is by itself healthy and holds Divine energy, but its energy can be multiplied with your own intention. Then, as you consume the blessed water, it helps to detoxify negative energy from within.

a. Fill a glass of water, and then hold it with both hands.

b. Speak to the water and direct it.

"As I consume you, may you cleanse my being and remove any negative thoughts, emotions and energies from inside and out. With the help of my lighted Angels, you are not blessed and holly."

c. Imagine white light emitting from your hands and into the water. Now drink and know that it will fulfill its purpose.

7. HOW TO GROUND YOURSELF

Even if you are not aware of the purpose of grounding, you can easily get the gist of it, simply with the name of the word: GROUND-ING. Trees are powerful and get all their energy from mother earth. Their roots ground inside earth, and so they grow, feed, and empower with nature's energy. Similar to the tree, you hold a bond with nature. Nature draws to you, with gravity; you have invisible roots that keep you close to earth.

Being connected to nature as a physical being has many benefits. One of the most important is energy. Physical bodies need nature's energy to empower, similar to a tree, to be strong. You need to be in sync with your own physical body, to control it, to feel good in it. Since you are not only physical bodies but spirits that have a body, earth helps you connect with your earthly body.

When you dream, or when you are in a deep meditative state, or when you astral project, your mind wonders and leaves your physical body. When you come back, in the first few seconds that you regain consciousness, you feel disoriented. This is because your spirit is not yet adjusted or grounded to your physical body and to the material world. For this, you might feel dizzy or lightheaded. This is when grounding is important.

If you enjoy meditation or astral projection, don't overdo it as you need spent time in your physical body as well. If you spent more time traveling with your soul, then you will have a hard time adjusting to your reality. Remember, you are in this physical world for a reason.

Grounding means gaining more energy through nature. You can do it anytime for empowerment and rejuvenation, to be more control of your body and to heal faster. If you get dizzy often, disoriented, out of focus, forgetful, sick, weak, or out of energy, it is time for some grounding.

WAYS TO GROUND:

1. Connect with nature. This is self-explanatory. Grounding has to do with merging your energy with nature and empowering from it, therefore, anything that has to do with nature grounds you. Gardening, walking barefoot on the ground, sitting under a tree, are some of the many ways that help you find balance between soul and body.

2. Be in the present moment. What is a more powerful way to ground, than the present moment? Stop and observe what is happening around you: the breeze on your hair, the cold book or tablet in your hands, the temperature in the room, the people in the house, the sounds that you hear. Notice all the things that exist in the present. Take them in, appreciate them; they are there for you.

3. Eat vegetables and fruit, drink water. As they come from earth, their energy helps to ground you. Also giving nutrition to your physique will help to balance the healthy energy within.

4. Crystals for grounding. Yes, crystals again, they have a lot of qualities and since they are part of nature; they hold parts of its energy. Simply hold a crystal, or put it next to you to help you ground back to the physical.

Some crystals with this quality are: hematite, smoky quartz, obsidian, red coral, black tourmaline, ruby, garnet, pyrite, onyx, tiger iron and black opal. For a complete list on crystals go to chapter 3.

5. Aromatherapy. Nature's gifts to us, once more. Some essential oils help us to be in sync with our environment. Enjoy their natural scent and empower.

For this purpose choose: Cedar wood, vetiver, benzoin, myrrh, sandal wood, cypress, oak moss, patchouli oil, rosewood, chamomile, elemi. For a complete list on essential oils, and for ways to use them, go to chapter 2.

6. Chant Om. Remember in a previous chapter we talked about this powerful Om chanting? Chant it and pay attention to the vibrations that the sounds make on your throat, and the effect they have on your body.

Here is a link to an Om chanting, sing along:
https://www.youtube.com/watch?v=HLhld_L1WBA

7. Grounding visualization. Find a quiet place, and clear your schedule for the next 7-10 minutes.

a. Close your eyes and breathe deeply in, hold your breath for 3 seconds and then out.

b. As you repeat the process four times, try to experience the power of the earth. With each in breath, you consume oxygen that is part of earth's energy.

c. Now put your attention on your feet, see earth's connection with your physical body. Imagine roots, similar to a tree, coming out of your soles and connecting to the ground. Feel the power that these roots emit and how you absorb earth's energy.

d. You are now similar to a tree that uses the energy of the earth to empower; with this you become stronger, grounded.

8. Move. Use your physical body in order to connect with it. Feel alive, dance, do yoga, jog.

9. Bath with salt. If you don't have time for a bath in the ocean, fill your bathtub. Use three handfuls of sea salt or Himalayan salt. If you don't have a tub, wash with a special salt body scrub.

8. HOW TO CENTER

Centering is being in control of all that you are. It is gaining the spiritual and physical power of your mind and body. To center, you bring yourself back to focus, put things in perspective, acknowledge your path and understand the inspiration that comes from Ether. In other words you are in control, at peace with yourself and your surroundings. When you are centered, you are able to make beneficial decisions, find your path, and enjoy life the most.

The following techniques are also powerful when you have panic attacks, or your days are filled with stress.

WAYS TO CENTER:

1. Pause. There may be a lot of things happening lately and perhaps you feel out of focus. There is no decision that needs to be made immediately, allow yourself time to step back for a while. When you do, you see things from a different perspective, you understand the reason behind those events, and you notice Divine guidance and resolution. Take a weekend getaway, go on a trip, clear your schedule for a day to relax. As you loosen up, things will begin to fall into place.

2. **Focus on your breathing.** This is a relaxation method especially for stress. When you focus on breathing, you calm down and you get to then see maters in a new light.

a. Close your eyes and breathe deeply.

b. As you focus on your breathing, notice your physical body. Notice the way it moves with each breath, notice how comfortable you feel.

c. Notice your emotions. You are feeling more and more relaxed and your stress is vanishing.

3. **Add energy to your "physical center of gravity".** This is the center of your physical energy; it exists under your navel area, or below your belly button. It is the center of your body and just focusing on that area, it helps to center the energy to your whole body.

a. Close your eyes and bring your attention on that area.

b. Now see the energy that surrounds this are.

c. Feel its power, its energy. With your attention in this area, you feel more centered almost immediately.

4. **Meditate**. Of course this is effective; don't question the power of some quiet time with yourself.

5. **Visualization**. Make a few moments to be in quiet.

a. Imagine the sky. See it as vividly as possible, the sky is your own state of mind. If you are stressful or sad, the sky is cloudy. See the grey clouds, just like before a rain. Feel that the clouds are your own emotions.

b. Be ready to remove those clouds/emotions. See them vanishing away. As they dissolve, you see the sunlight and finally, the bright sun. Feel the light of the sun warming up your soul.

9. HOW TO BRING POSITIVE ENERGY IN YOUR HOME / Feng Shui

As this is a basic guide, I will give a general idea of easy things to do to bring positive energy into your home. The main goal of this list is to purify the energy, attract lighted beings in your home, and welcome the high frequency of well-being, inspiration, joy and abundance.

Handling the energy of your home is an art, and many people have studied it and named it: Feng shui. This focuses on the energy of the objects, their color and their position.

Certain elements hold purer energy than others, and they affect your own energy as you share the same space. Objects absorb energy from their environment. The positive or negative attention they receive whenever someone observes them makes a particular object receive that energy, and then shares it accordingly to the people around them. Imagine how you would feel when you enter an old, unclean space with ugly objects versus a new furnished and well decorated room with beautiful colors. The observations and emotions you receive, get imprinted in the space and its objects.

Feng shui has to do with how your environment affects your energy and concentration. A messy desk with piles of papers for instance, causes you to lose things and brings the energy of disorientation and chaos in your work space and job itself.

Additionally, certain colors provide peace while others extra energy. Certain symbols, elements and objects bring empowerment or introduce a variety of different benefits. Some are used for financial growth while others for health and so on. Be aware however, that too much information is added and altered as time progresses and there's no need to go by every detail according to feng shui experts. In other words you don't have to do anything that you read in a feng shui guide book, as that would be unnecessary and stressing for you. Make changes to your home by trusting your intuition as it will guide you to the changes you need to make.

Relax, clear your mind and ask the Angels to reveal to you any changes that you need to make in each room. Usually you will notice something, or someone will make a remark, or even you will receive the inspiration to change or make a change.

I enlist the most important steps to help you get started, there are many more feng-shui tips and guides that you can study separately. However, I do believe that you should trust your intuition more than a feng-shui guide.

WAYS TO ENHANCE POSITIVE ENERGY IN YOUR HOME

1. **Clear your space from clutter and old objects.** Remember don't keep anything that you do not like, instead replace it or transform it to something you enjoy looking at.

2. **A good idea is to add some crystals around your house.** They help to absorb any negative energy and purify your environment.

3. **Burn some essential oils regularly**, or find some essential oil deodorant to purify the energy of the air.

4. **Add fresh plants**. If you have any sick or dead plants, they emanate negative energy. Replace them with healthy ones. Add some fresh plants on your entrance. They welcome good vibrations.

5. **Redecorate**. As mentioned above, remove anything that you don't like from your space, and add your own delicate touches. If you find something beautiful, then it has positive energy.

6. **Relocate furniture.** Change Is good, if you feel that the energy of your home is stuck, then you alter it by moving some furniture around.

7. **Throw away the trash, and fix anything broken**. This goes without saying, broken objects and trash equals negative energy.

8. **Place high energy objects.** There are certain objects that contain high energy. This may be images of nature, some statues like mother Mary, or even laughing Buddha are considered positive. You can also put some mandala images or symbols of wealth. Also images of nature and oceans help to raise the energy.

9. **Color**. Colors have their own vibrations. If you add some light colors in your home, you allow them to lighten your space. Consider light colors like yellow, light blue, light green, pink, purple, gold.

10. **Fountains**. You bring in water which combines movement and entails moving energy. The same as the blood in your veins it moves and helps you to be healthy. The water helps the energy "recycle". Also add some drops of essential oil in the water.

11. **Tidy**. This is important, if you have piles of magazines and books laying around, old boxes and so on, you stuff in extra energy and that is not healthy.

12. **Open windows regularly.** Allow the fresh oxygen to bring in high vibrational energy.

13. **Let sunshine in**. sun has powerful uplifting energy. Let it in often.

14. **Mirror**, mirror on the wall… They are a wealth magnet. They reflect the light and multiply it. They represent new pathways, opportunities and abundance. Place some mirror in your favorite rooms to extend their good energy.

15. **Aquarium**. Water element equals good flow and wealth. Place a pretty aquarium in your living room or office room.

10. HOW TO PURIFY YOUR FOOD

Anything has energy, even the food you consume. Whatever you eat, you absorb its energy that it then matches with your own.

Some foods contain higher energy than others; those help us become more energetic, more focused and revived. Unfortunately, the majority of the foods has been handled by others, has been processed, and contains processed features, or if it is animal it has been violently slaughtered. Those kinds of foods block our energy, makes us feel drained and out of focus. The good news is that we can easily distinguish between the two.

High vibrational foods come from earth, have nothing or little processing and are handled with care and love. Those foods consist of high vibrations and nature's energy. Additionally, imagine a chicken hut, in the mountains with the chickens running free and handled by your grandmother, versus chickens that are raised in a dirty warehouse, they barely see the sun and ultimately get violently slaughtered. What sort of energies will the two have? Within the meat they hold their energy, either that was fear and pain or happiness and fulfillment. Unfortunately most of the meat that comes from stores consists of low energy meat.

Similarly, processed food alters the energy of a product that we then consume. Think of brown sugar versus the alternative to sugar, think of fresh juice versus juice from a box. In this way, you can easily distinguish which products have high vibrational energy, and which ones will block our own.

Food addictions also block our energy and thus our inspiration, creativity and connection. Anything that you consume in a regular basis such as coffee and sugar for instance, or even smoking, they are processed and limit our energy.

If you want to expand your spirituality, or channel spirit, be extra careful what you consume.

Thankfully, the Angels have guided me to an easy process to raise the levels of energy of any kind of food before you consume it. Of course, this does not mean that any negative energy is erased, or that the food will transform from low energy to high, but it will help to eliminate excessive negative energy from it.

STEPS TO PURIFY YOUR FOOD

This technique works for both food and drinks. I suggest you follow it before you consume each meal.

1. With the food or drink in front of you invoke high energy to cleanse and empower it.

"I lovingly call forth any loving spirit that can most assist, please come forth and purify my food. Remove any negative energy that it may contain, and raise its purity so it gives me great health and high vibration. Thank for helping me, I love you so, and so it is."

2. Raise your hand towards the food or drink, and imagine white light emanating from your hand to the food. Imagine it glowing with that energy. Count to five, and then lower your hand.

3. Talk to the food: "I ask that you transform into well-being, nutrition and high energy once consumed. Thank you, and so it is."

Your food or drink is now ready to be consumed. Remember to appreciate each bite and notice all the taste that it brings. It is there to serve you, and you are there to enjoy it.

11. HOW TO USE A TIBETANT BOWL

Recent studies acknowledge the benefits of sound therapy. Certain frequencies affect our brains by giving out certain vibrations. You have heard of theta waves for instance. This is a frequency that helps us reach high relaxation. The Tibetan bowl sound, does not include theta waves, however its sound is special. It helps to clear away negative energy, and as we pay attention to it, we clear away thoughts making it a perfect ally for our meditation. Likewise, the Tibetan bowl is a perfect tool to use before any channelings, as it clears the energy of your space and generates a relaxed state of mind, ready for channeling spirit.

When you ring the Tibetan bowl, it creates a bell sound that echoes in lower frequency that establishes a calming effect. This technique is originated from India, and used in Buddhist practices, but it is not considered a sacred method. It is usually used for meditation, well-being, relaxation, to invite pure energy into your being, and for healing. It is believed that the sound frequency of the bowl restores any abnormality in the aura and creates harmony.

The Tibetan bowl sounds, usually causes an instant centering effect. The tones create harmonization of our left and right brain. Meditating on its sounds tunes one in to the universal sound of our existence.

STEPS TO USING THE TIBETAN BOWL:

The process of using this technique is very easy. The Tibetan bowl contains two items, the bowl itself, usually metal, and a wooden mallet.

1. Hold the singing bowl on the palm of the left hand.

2. Hold the mallet with all the fingertips pointing downwards, and touching the middle of the mallet.

3. Gently tap the mallet against the side of the bowl.

4. With an equal density, rub the mallet clockwise around the outside edge of the bowl. Use a full arm movement and rotate your arm with the mallet. Again, it's not a wrist movement, but a full-arm movement. Do the clockwise movement several times and then let go, enjoying the echo.

5. Repeat for as long as you need.

12. HOW TO NATURALY RELEASE STRESS

We all get those moments of fury, panic or anxiety. As much as we want to remain calm, something causes us to worry. In situations like these, it is better to relax and not add to the negative emotion. The following techniques will help you gain control in those moments you feel you are losing control of your emotions.

WAYS TO RELEASE STRESS, PANIC, ANXIETY:

1. **Visualize a positive outcome.** Whatever has caused those negative emotions, there is always a way it can be resolved. Your future is not yet written, and your time right now is all you need to create it the way you want it. By stressing out, you cause a negative outcome, so relax, and know that everything will be alright, because honestly, it really will.

Close your eyes and see the event as it is happening right now the way you want it resolved. Muster as much positive energy you have left and add it in that image. The more time you spent on it, the more it will make you feel better, and the more you create that outcome.

2. **Angel assistance.** Angels are always around whenever you call for them. They can help you release stress and make everything better. If you are spiritual, you may feel their presence immediately with you.

"I call upon the most loving and lighted Angels, to surround me now, and help me release any negative emotions, as well as resolve the event that has upset me. Surround me with your loving light and embrace me with your love. I need you now, and I know you are with me wherever I call. For this I thank you from the bottom of my heart. Thank you, thank you, thank you."

3. **Appreciation.** A great way to calm down is to name as may things as you can that make you feel grateful. As you think of them, you notice that you have so many great things in your life, and whatever has caused you to be upset, does not seem that important anymore.

4. **Singing bowl.** If you have a singing bowl, you are lucky. Similar to crystals, the sound of this singing bowl helps to remove negative energy from our aura that eventually soothes us.

5. **Aromatherapy**. Some essential oils bring the relaxing effect and help us remove stress. Have some of the following essential oils handy for moments like that: amyris, bargamond, Chamomile, cinnamon, Frankincense, wintergreen.

13. HOW TO NATURALY HEAL A HEADACHE

Pills mess with your body, mind and energy. Before rushing to swallow a pill every time you have a headache, try one of those methods first.

Headache, the same with anything else, is formed through energy. Whenever you absorb negative energy through your attention, eyes, sounds or thoughts, it is stored up in your crown chakra and prevents the natural flow of your energy. The natural result of this grey energy causes you dizziness, pain or the annoying effect of a headache. We all get them and so I have asked the Angels to share with us ways to remove them easily and efficiently. The good news is that since headache is but energy, we can discard it by using the ways below. Some ways might work better than others for some, so do experiment.

WAYS TO REMOVE HEADACHE:

1. **Crystals:** I will not be going into the healing techniques of crystals, since that needs another book by an experienced crystal healer practitioner. The information I get from my guides however, is that certain crystals absorb negative energy and for this I present the following steps:

> **a**. Decide which crystal you will be using. For healing and absorbing dark energies I recommend: Selenite, Amethyst, clear quartz.

> **b**. Cleanse and energize your crystal. Reference chapter 3.

> **c**. Program your crystals and direct them to absorb the negative energy. Reference chapter 3 for crystal programming.

> **d**. Relax and simply place your crystal on your forehead, or the side of your head that is in pain.

> **e**. Allow your crystal to work as you relax and meditate for around thirty minutes, or until you feel that the headache has dissolved.

2. **Meditate:** As you relax and let go of bothering thoughts, your energies flow more easily. I suggest you meditate on the Um mantra, (chapter 17) or some soothing sounds.

3. **Theta waves:** as you listen to this certain frequency, energy spreads and expands and you can throw any dark energy out of your energy field. Find some great theta wave audios online, and remember to use your headphones.

4. Intention: my guides are telling me, "your intention is your greatest ally."

> **a.** Speak these words: "my headache is beginning to dissolve and it will be completely gone within the next few minutes." Believe this statement, as your intention and determination orders the energies to work for you.

> **b.** Visualize white healing light surrounding your head. This light is expanding your aura and releases any dark energy from your energy.

5. TIBETAN BOWL: you use the sound of this bowl to cleanse dark energy from your crystals. In the same way, you use it to remove dark energy from your aura. Reference chapter 11 on how to work with Tibetan bowl.

6. Angel Healing: I love to call Archangel Raphael for a quick healing. I have tried it before and my headaches and any other kind of pain, was completely removed. Thank you so much Archangel Raphael.

> *"I call upon Archangel Raphael, to release me from this headache. I lovingly ask you to surround me with your powerful healing light and restore my energy to health. Thank you, and so it is."*

7. SALT BATH: Natural salt has a cleansing technique. We use it to cleanse negative energy out of crystals. Similarly, if you take a salt bath, it will absorb negative energy and purify your aura. As your aura clears, the healing rays of your aura are restored and so the headache seizes. I include a few salt bath recipes to help you maximize the healing effect.

RECIPE:

Handful of Epsom salts

1 teaspoon baking soda, to soften waters and avoid skin irritation

10 drops of Essential oil of chamomile or rosemary

8. **Nature:** Sit under a tree and focus on your breathing. You absorb in energy from earth that replaces any false energy from your aura. You rejuvenate.

Headache is a normal symptom of spiritual enhancement. When your crown chakra becomes bigger, or your third eye opens, headache comes as a consequence effect and it may last a few days.

14. HOW TO INTERPRET YOUR DREAMS

When you sleep your unconscious mind takes over. Whatever you have stored with your memories, interactions and thoughts, it makes its way outwards, through your dreams.

Your remember those confusing, interesting dreams that mix and match with various people and events that do not make much sense. Those thoughts and ideas do not bring any message to you but work through your subconscious in order to be released from your memory. To be removed, they first pass through your attention to release their energy and any impact they may have on you. Therefore, do not try to make sense of those uninteresting random dreams because not all are important. There are those however that try to bring you a message and this is what I focus on in this section.

As every person is different, they have various experiences, memories and interactions and therefore, the way they interpret any event is different based on their perceptions and memories. For this, dreams are explained differently from one to the other, so you cannot rely on those dream interpretations books to understand your own dreams.

The truth is that any dream that tries to convey a message comes through in such a way in order to be understood by you. The same message for instance, to another person will come through completely differently. The dreams, come to you in such a way because you have your own way to interpret them, based on your experiences, perceptions and memories. But let's discuss the main question you are thinking right now. Who brings those messages?

As you rest, your ego is finally silenced, and you are open to Divine communication. The truth is, you can gain Divine communication whenever you quiet your mind, however, when you sleep you let go of fears, concerns and doubts and any loving spirit can easily pass on their messages to you. Usually dreams that bring a message, derive from your spiritual team. Your spiritual team is a set of lighted beings like spirit guides and guardian Angels, helping you from the Ether. This team tries to help you reach your desires and your life's path; it brings you guidance, assistance, inspiration and ease. Didn't you ever get a great idea, when you were sleeping? Or you finally remembered what you were trying to remember a few hours ago? Perhaps you finally understand a question that someone asked, or a solution to a problem. This is may occur later because your team helped you out. They knew you were thinking about it, trying to remember, or what you need help with, either a new project, a new idea, a solution, and so they bring it to you when you pay attention the most, when you are about to drift to slip, or through your subconscious dreams.

But how do you interpret those dreams? Follow the easy guide below and don't worry if you are not sure at first, with practice you will get better at knowing what is right.

STEPS TO INTERPRET YOUR DREAMS:

1. Write the dream down, as soon as you wake up. This way you don't forget any vital details. As soon as you wake up, your subconscious is still active. When the conscious is fully awake, you may block those dreams.

2. Set your intention first:

"I intend to fully capture the message of this dream as it was given to me in my sleep. I ask my spiritual team to help me understand it. Thank you, and so it is."

3. Did the dream make somewhat sense to you? Was it vivid? Meaningful? Did you have a strong emotion as you were experiencing it? If not, this may be one of those dreams that is random and not important. When this happens, relax knowing that whatever happened in the dream does not need interpretation.

4. Are you the protagonist in the dream or are you observing another? If the dreams were not happening to you, then perhaps it was intended for you to help that person, or pass on the message.

5. Make a list of the people in your dream and what they mean to you. For instance did you see your mother? What emotions does this person bring to you? Write them down. If you didn't recognize the people, or you don't remember who they were, try to remember how they made you feel, then associate them with a person that makes you feel that way. The message is mostly connected to them.

6. Do you have a sense, a knowing what this message might be? Give it a thought now, connect the people and events in the dream and try to find what they might mean to YOU. Do not associate them with any universal dream interpretations. If you saw a dog for instance, try to find out what that animal means to you? A companion, a friend? Perhaps it means time to play, have fun; or even it shows you someone that is genuinely happy to be around.

7. What was the event that occurred? For instance if you were dreaming of a dog, consider if the dog was sad in the dream, or ill? Then perhaps you are missing some time to relax and play, or you feel the need to connect with someone that understands and is happy to see you. Your spiritual team helps you to understand this through a dream.

8. Make a list of all possible dream interpretations and now follow your intuition. Which one do you feel it is for you? You can never be wrong, since you know the answer already.

- Your spiritual team guides those dreams through your own experiences, memories, knowledge and emotions. You are the only one able to solve the dream interpretations.

- Dreams also include many settings from our other past lives. As your subconscious travels through time, you recognize settings within the dreams, but you don't remember them, or they seemed unexplainable to you, once you awake. Such dreams may be your ability to fly. In the dream you were flying, and you knew how to do it. This was possibly a skill you acquired in another life.

- Also on the subject of past lives, many nightmares may also come out in this way, as a bad experience you went through in another life. My fiancé for instance, when a child, he kept having the same recurring dream, of being sucked in by a tornado. He was in the tornado, he was swirling along with many objects and feeling terrified. Possibly, this was a past life experience, that was imprinted in the subconscious wanting to be released.

- Sometimes your lost loved ones sent you dreams to soothe you. Nightmares are not intended to be scary. Those dreams that bring messages might have gotten out of hand and got confused by your ego self that misinterpret the messages and brought you frightening thoughts. An example of this is from my own experience. As a child I kept having the same dream that my father was still alive and living in the house with us. The dream came every year and every time I seemed to recognize it while dreaming but did not remember it when I woke up. In the dream there was a woman wearing black or grey clothes and stood near him whenever he went. Neither of them talked, nor looked at us.

In the dream I was confused and I was asking my mother in the dream what was my father doing in the house with us. As the dream was guided by spirit they chose the one person I was most comfortable with to explain.

"It is normal, your dad misses us and he asked Mother Mary

to bring him every year so he can see us."

As a teenager I was terrified of spirits and ghosts. As soon as I realized what was happening my ego began to send fear to me and I woke up scared in the middle of the night frightened that I wasn't alone. Such a beautiful soothing dream, yet the ego holds our fears, so as I began to awake, the ego kicked in and fear took over.

Fear years later and as I crafted spirit communication I connected with my father and he said: "It wasn't my intention to scare you". Of course not, I did that, not him.

Needless to say, I didn't have that dream again.

15. HOW TO USE MANDALAS

Mandalas are patterns with geometric and earth symbols, formed together in one to produce an energetic artwork. They are formed out of symmetric pieces. Their pattern, color and chemistry produce different spiritual results.

Usually these symbols are handled differently, and cause different results to each one. To use mandalas, and notice their effect you must craft the ability to connect with them. The same with almost anything, the more you practice, the more you enhance your craft and hence their powers take more effect. Yes, mandalas do hold power. Their power comes from their symmetry, patterns, intention of the creator and pure energy that is added to them.

Special symbols, lock together the intention of the artist, the capture the energy of a kind spirit that helps to create it, it stores it and empowers the person who uses them. Their powers may entail: release of blockages, inspiration, spiritual connection, a vision as an answer, or enhancement of your spiritual cord.

Usually mandalas are part of a spiritual artwork. A mandala is not created as a whole idea in the mind of the artist beforehand, but it is inspired symbol by symbol. The formation is in other words guided by spirit. For reference on how to create spiritual artwork, see chapter 51.

Below I list the steps that you can work with mandalas, assuming that you have one at hand. The process in choosing a ready mandala is similar to the one of a crystal. You don't choose it, it chooses you. The one that spots your eye is the one that it will help you the most. If it finds you, if it is a gift, or you see it anywhere, it is also not a coincidence, but it appears itself to you. On the other hand, if you want to have a special mandala created for you by an artist, then spirit will guide the artist to form the best mandala for you at that time.

You work with mandalas in order to capture their essence. So, once you have your mandala, begin following with the following steps.

STEPS TO WORK WITH MANDALAS:

I. Take some breaths and relax your mind. Let go of any expectations. If you have a physical drawing, hold the mandala in your hand; if you only have a digital mandala in front of you, and then just stare at the screen. Usually, the intention unlocks the energy from the mandala and transmutes it onto the state in your mind or out loud:

> *"I release the energy of this mandala, to affect me in the most positive way. I allow its energy to work with me now, so as to gain its good effects. Thank you and so it is."*

If you want the mandala to give you a specific outcome, then just hold the intention of the end result.

This first step is to unlock its energy, and to allow it to work with you. Usually, if a mandala is associated with an Angel or any spirit, this step will allow them to assist you.

1. Get in a relaxed position and stare at the mandala in front of you. Let go of any distractions and thoughts, and fixate on its colors, patterns, symbols. Notice all the details and you will soon begin be in a meditative state.

2. Notice any ideas, thoughts, visions or inspiration as the mandala gives you spiritual enhancement. According to the mandala, the effects will differ. Similarly, every time you use it, you may get different results.

Instead of meditating on a mandala, you can also sketch or paint one, for similar effects.

The steps are simple, but the more you work with a mandala, the more you get to the center of its energy. Many of the mandalas work as an alternative to meditation; since they help you connect with your higher Divinity.

16. HOW TO FEEL ENERGY

This chapter is mainly created for those that prefer tangible proof of spiritual processes. Energy, similar to spirit, is invisible to the untrained eye. The good news is you can train your eye to both see and feel energy. Since you are still in the beginner's section of this book, the easier method is to feel energy. This will also help you believe of the power of the universe and understand how easily you can summon and use it.

Everything that exists has energy. Ideas, objects, crystals, animals, trees, words also have energy. Your thoughts recall energy, your words summon it. Your chakras are sources that contain energy. In order to feel, as physical beings, we use our hands. Our hands contain chakras that keep and send out energy. Think of them as portals of giving and transmitting energy.

Many people experience energy differently. Some feel light electricity, warmth, cold spots, heaviness, pressure, softness and many more. For the means of this method, keep an open mind and watch out for any changes in your hands.

This technique is to simply train your hands to feel energy.

STEPS TO FEEL ENERGY:

METHOD 1:

1. Relax, clear you mind and set the intention to feel energy in your hands.

2. To help your hands relax and get ready to receive energy, visualize a white light surrounding your hands "activating" them.

3. Work your muscles of your hands; move them thoroughly to help your energy move through your body. Exercise your fingers and wrists for a few seconds.

4. Raise your left or right palm and pay attention to how it feels right now. Move it to see how light it is and that there is not any sort of pressure on it. This will help to compare the difference in the following step.

5. Now summon energy. Let's summon the energy of an apple. With your hand raised as if you are holding an apple, imagine a big apple in your hand. Now say the word three times out loud: "apple, apple, apple."

6. Move your hand slowly and notice the pressure in your palm. You have created the energy of an apple that now feels as heavy as if you are actually holding one! With your other hand try to feel the apple. Notice the pressure when you try to bring your two palms together.

Your thoughts and words have created the energy of an apple. Now it's possible that its energy will follow you around until it has actually manifested in physical apple in front of you. If you notice an apple in the next few hours, it is your own energy that has summoned it forth!

Reference chapter 21, Law of attraction, on steps to manifest your desires, as energy works in the same way.

METHOD 2:

1. Relax, clear you mind and set the intention to feel energy in your hands.

2. To help your hands relax and get ready to receive energy, visualize a white light surrounding your hands "activating" them.

3. Work your muscles of your hands; move them to help your energy move through your body.

4. Cup your hands close together, as if holding a small ball. Hold the intention of creating an energy ball between your hands.

5. Move your hands slowly front and back of each other. This way you are creating an energy ball with the energy of your hands. Slowly make the space between your hands bigger. Craft the energy ball as long as it needs until you feel it between your hands.

6. Feel the energetic ball you have created in between your hands. How does it feel? As I have tried it myself right now, it feels like a breeze in between my hands. With my trained eye, I see the energy ball I have created as light yellow. Experience this ball of energy and try to see its energy as well. It helps to have a white background to notice energy.

You may notice heaviness, electricity, heat, breeze as some of the indications of invisible energy.

17. HOW TO USE MANTRAS

Mantra can be a syllable, a word or a phrase that you repeat over and over. Some mantras are powerful because they are used to summon forth certain energy that works as an attractor of what you desire. For instance, there are mantras for wealth for instance, to attract prosperity flow in your life, for love, power and so forth.

The mantras were originally used in India. The reason that these mantras are powerful is not because they are magical or sacred. They are associated with certain "gods" or "goddesses" or "spirits" that they invoked to help summon forth that energy. As with anything, the more you repeat or think of something, the bigger momentum it creates. They are like prayers that are accompanied by powerful spirits to help us access the desirable energy.

With mantras, we summon forth energy that has been stored in that mantra and along with it Spiritual assistance.

To use a mantra it is important to know what you are trying to achieve. Either that is wealth, protection, success, spiritual connection. A mantra needs to be repeated several times, consciously. To benefit from its energy, you must use the mantra sounds correctly, and listen to the sound of your voice as you repeat them, or the vibrations its' sounds create.

The combination of sounds put together, makes each mantra unique and "locks" energy within it. When you repeat the mantra you "unlock" its energy that it links to your own, or to your space, according to your intention.

Mantras are quite powerful and do not need to be repeated daily or even for long to benefit from their power.

You can listen to a mantra or chant it. I like to meditate on mantras as well. When you have a certain note or mantra in your mind, no other thought interrupts your meditation. Also mantras hold the right sounds to balance your body and mind, help you relax and connect with Spiritual forces. They also help to clear out any karmic issues.

Similar to crystals, you choose the mantra that you feel most drawn to. You have to be ready for it and not blocking its energy. To understand if a mantra is the right one for you repeat it several times and notice if your energy gets affected in any way. Every time I use the mantra "Om" for instance I feel deeply relaxed, and get in a meditative state almost instantly. I then know that it is indeed very powerful mantra for me.

If a mantra used to empower you after a while you notice that is has no more effect, you have probably captured all the assistance it can give you for that time. Similarly, a mantra that wasn't powerful to you before, you may notice that it affects you in a positive manner later on. This is because your thoughts and energy change all the time.

I have created a collection of powerful mantras you can use, but I suggest you also study the sound they make to make sure you chant them correctly.

When you chant mantras, think or visualize your desires as already manifested.

To notice results working with mantras I suggest you choose a mantra that resonates with you and chant it 3 x 21 times in the morning and 3 x 21 at night for 20 days.

MANTRAS

1. **OM or AUM:** Cleansing, meditation, spiritual connection

2. **Om Namah Shivaya:** self-confidence, inner power, bliss, peace

Om Saha Naavavatu

Saha Nau Bhunaktu

Saha Veeryam Karavaavahai

Tejasvi Aavadheetamastu Maa Vidvishaavahai Om

This is a powerful mantra for restoration, balance, success in new projects and businesses

3. **Om Hreem Shreem Lakshmibhayo Namah:** for wealth, success

4. **Soham:** Breathe in "So" breath out "Ham" for relaxation.

5. **Hari Om:** Energy flow, removes blockages

6. **Maha Ganapati Mool:** Removes obstacles, brings success

7. **Mahamrityunjaya:** Health, wealth, long life, rejuvenation

8. **Ap sahee hoa sache da sache dhoa, har, har, har:** Mantra for prosperity

9. Tayata Om Bekanze Bekanze Maha Bekanze Radza Samudgate Soha: success, freedom

10. Jehi Vidhi Hoi Naath Hit Moraa Karahu So Vegi Daas Main Toraa: success, brings opportunities

11. **Sat Nam**: truth, inspiration

12. **Wahe Guru:** raises vibration

13.**Om Gum Ganapatayei Namah**: Protection, attracts good opportunities

14. **om shrim hrim klim mahalakshimi yei namaha**: prosperity, abundance

15. **Om a ra pa ca na dhih:** for wisdom, to improve skills

16. **Om vajrapani hum**: forgiveness

17. **Aham Aarogyam**: health, power

18. HOW TO INVOKE SPIRITS, ANGELS, AND ASCENTED MASTERS

The word 'invoke" may suggest, calling forth, asking for assistance, praying over, or simply talking with. You don't need to have any important reason to invoke spirits, Angels or ascended masters. They are always available, and they can be in many places at once. You don't need to worry that you may be bothering them; they are always eager and grateful to help you.

Every time you invoke a spirit, they come forth. You may not be able to see or feel them, but they know they have been called. If they cannot assist you, they summon another spirit that can to help you with what you are asking.

You can use the following techniques to summon any spirit, no matter if they are a lost loved one, a spirit guide, or an ascended master. The key to spirit invocation is intention.

STEPS TO INVOKE SPIRIT:

1. Decide the reason of this invocation first. Is it to ask for help, to send gratitude, to ask for protection?

2. Choose which spirit you wish to invoke. If you want protection for instance, you may call for Archangel Michael, if you want healing, Archangel Raphael, or Jesus. If you ask for support, then mother Mary, or your very own spirit guide. If you wish to receive enlightenment and inspiration, ask for your guardian Angel and so forth.

3. In your mind, out loud, or even in writing, speak to the spirit telling it the reason of this invocation. Be present as you do this, and always have your intention in mind. Know that you are heard at all times.

There is no fancy way to invoke spirit, not any specific words that you should speak. They know and respond at all times, as your intention foretells what you are thinking.

A very powerful method is to bring your awareness towards the spirit you want to call. If it is a lost loved on, remember them clearly, if it is an Angel, try to tune into their divinity as you call out their name three times.

4. Whatever you have asked for, the spirits work to assist you. If you have asked for clearing, protection, or even sign and answers, they try to respond. This might happen immediately. For this, step four, is to pay attention. The answer comes in many ways. If you asked for a sign, notice in what ways it may come. You may sense warmth, tingling sensation, a shine, a reassuring thought. If you want clearing or protection, trust that it is done. If you ask for guidance, notice it as it comes through your own intuition, inspiration and watch out for new opportunities.

5. Thank spirit for coming forth to assist you.

- Not all wishes or prayers are met. By invoking spirit don't think that they are a genie making all your wishes come true. They cannot intervene with the world, nor sent you a bundle of wealth if you ask. What they can do, is guide you to get it yourself.

- Also they cannot make someone do something because you have asked them to. They never intervene with anyone else's free will. They can however help you heal faster, or protect someone for you.

- You can of course ask for your diseased loved, one. If on the other hand, you don't have anyone in particular in mind, you can focus on the purpose of this invocation, and the most helpful spirit, will come forth to assist you.

- Many wish to speak to God and that is acceptable as well. God may then send an appropriate spirit or Angel to assist.

- You should know that usually spirits appear in groups. If you ask for clearing for instance, a team of helpful guides may step forth to assist.

19. HOW TO COMMUNICATE WITH SPIRIT THROUGH MEDITATION

There are many ways to connect with spirit directly to receive guidance, answers to your questions and empowerment. This includes using divination tools, psychic abilities, channeling, or meditation.

You can connect with spirit while in a meditative state as then you let go of your conscious mind, and along with it, thoughts, judgment and ego. This way, it is easier to receive guidance, understand and accept it.

There is not a particular skill needed to connect with your guides through meditation. You have to be ready to receive their guidance, and you have crafted the skill to quiet your mind enough, to go into a meditative state.

Many people use this technique as a way to communicate with their spiritual team, and receive insight to their problems. While using this technique, spirit will come forth and connect with you, by transmitting high energy, emotions, words and/ or imagery. Part of the imagery is from your imagination through memories, just to help you accept the messages you receive. That does not imply that if you see your spirit guide as woman, that it has actually has a female figure. They appear to you in a form that you are ready to accept, in order to open up to their guidance, and not be afraid. A beautiful female figure for instance, is a soothing image that they also relate to.

With that being said, many people perceive communication through a meditative state differently. Some may feel intense emotions, and knowing as an answer and others may get in a real-like conversation with spirit. In any case that connection is perceived, accept it. Every time you try this technique, you experience it differently. Also different spirits, choose to guide you in different settings, and in different ways.

Whenever you are ready for a real-like communication with spirit, and you have achieved a meditative state of relaxation before, (chapter 1) use the following steps.

STEPS FOR SPIRIT COMMUNICATION THROUGH MEDITATION

There are two ways this technique can occur. For the first one is find a guided meditation that helps you create the setting, and become ready for communication with your spirit guide, or any other spirit. For the purpose of assisting you, I am working on some guided meditations like this. Please check my website at: http://ameliabert.com/

For the second technique recreate such a setting with your imagination as I guide you below.

1. Get to your usual meditation routine, and put on some meditation music.

2. Ask for protection: "Archangel Michael of the light, I call upon you to embrace me with your Divine Light and shield me against any negative energies, thoughts, negative spirits and people. Thank you, and so it is."

3. Intention: *"I ask the most helpful spirit guide to connect with me through meditation, as clearly as I can perceive them, to guide, bring insight, and assist me to move forward in my life. Help me feel and see your energy in a form I can understand, help me to connect with you as clearly as possible so that I benefit from your presence. Thank you, and so it is."*

4. Try to be as relaxed as possible, and allow the images to form in your mind, without judgment. In this step, your guides will help you when you are ready to understand them. As explained before, you might listen to their words form in your mind, and / or see the images appear as from your own imagination. When your spirit comes forth, ask them any questions.

5. Visualize a doorway. Your guide awaits for you there. When you open the door you will find yourself in a beautiful setting. This might anything. When you are ready open the door and enter the setting. Ask your guides to meet you if they are not already there. When they do ask them anything you want.

6. As soon as you are finished, slowly regain consciousness and write down anything that you remember from your conversation.

This technique works best for a connection with your spirit guides. You can of course try to connect with a lost loved one, but know that their energy might not be strong enough to help you receive clear connection or even imagery.

20. HOW TO COMMUNICATE WITH A LOST LOVED ONE

There are several steps that the soul takes, once it is released from a physical body. One of them is to look after the ones they left behind, and make sure they let them know they are around.

Most spirits, acknowledge the pain that comes from their passing, and want to help their loved ones by easing their suffering. They try to send messages, reassurance, or signals to let them know they are around. Your part is to acknowledge them once they come.

Spirits wish for the well-being of all, they do not care for revenge or injustice, at least a 99% of them, returns to a pure state of love and happiness. They have to undergo expansion, and their path never ends. For this, they check up on us often, but they are not with us all the time after their passing. If you call them, they usually come, wanting to offer you ease and assistance.

In this chapter, I bring you the ways a spirit might connect with us. Channeling their words, or energy, requires a more skilled process, so the following list comes handy if you are not that skilled yet.

WAYS SPIRIT COMMUNICATES:

All souls use different ways of communication with us, usually based on their own skills. The older a soul, the more skilled it is, and it uses more unique ways to pass on their message. In this list, I include the most common ones.

1. **Warmth**. They shower their loved ones with an energy that feels warm to our physical skin. They want to reassure in that way that they love you, they are around, and to soothe your worry.

2. **Light**. Most souls are handy with using light to get our attention. Those glimpses of sparkle we sometimes get, it might come from spirit. Here, they want to get our attention on a specific item or idea, by showing us an item. They try to make us turn towards that item by sending sparkles of light to get our attention.

3. **Smell**. They often recreate a smell, to remind us of their presence. The creation of anything in the physical world is a handy skill usually used by more experienced spirits. Younger spirits, can guide us to the particular moment, or close to the area so we smell the essence they want us to receive. Usually that essence intrigues our memory and we associate it with them. For instance if you grandmother used to smell cookies, when you smell freshly baked cookies you remember her. Your grandmother knows this so she will guide you towards that smell.

4. **Sound**. You might have a song you two used to love, a special bell noise or any other kind of sound that it reminds you of them. They guide you to the time to perceive that sound, or music, in hopes that you associate it with them, to bring you reassurance.

5. **Tingling sensation.** They focus on one area of your body, and they sent part of their energy to be perceived as a soft touch on your skin. Usually, the areas they use to send their energy are meaningful as well.

6. I usually get this tingling sensation on my cheek every night I go to bed. They sent me their goodnight kisses.

7. **People**. Something someone said, reminded you of a lost loved one. That is not a coincidence, as they may have inspired people to say something, or act in a particular way so that you acknowledge the similarity. This often occurs with children, as they are more receptive.

8. **Animals**. Usually they sent parts of their energy, to an animal, to keep you company. How many times I heard the stories of a woman believing their dog is their lost husband. That might be very possible. It is also possible that part of their energy reincarnates as your pet.

9. **Children**. Like I mentioned before, children are very receptive, they can perceive an image, or the words of a spirit very easily. This occurs in hopes that the child will then transfer the messages back to you.

10. **Dreams**. As discussed in the chapter of dreams 14, when we sleep, we are more receptive with spirit. Our loved ones know this, and they use it as a time to bring forth messages. They appear in our dreams to soothe and assist us. You remember those dreams, as their purpose is to understand that it was their message to you from them.

11. **Knowing**. Yes, they can let us know they are with us from within. They help us accept that they are with us at any time, even if we cannot explain how we are so sure of it.

12. **Reincarnation**. Many times, a spirit wants to stay close to us, or continue on a similar path. For this, they often choose to reincarnate as a family member. If your grandchild or even child reminds you of your parent, or friend, there may be more to it.

- Spirits will never come to hurt, or frighten us. For this, you will almost never, see them with your physical eyes, or hear their voice externally.

- They respect our free will, and cannot intervene with our lives.

- They cannot be present with us all the time, since they too have expansion to undergo.

- Sometimes, spirits don't come for a visit. Perhaps they don't have the strength, or they have an important path to undergo. Know you will meet them again soon enough.

21. HOW TO ATTRACT DESIRABLE EVENTS

We are part energy. Everything around us is energy. There is energy outside of your bodies in our aura. Our words have energy, what we consume also has energy, what we do and think also has energy. To bring forth that energy, all you have to do is think energy. Nothing is too big to have or desire since all is part of the same energy. A dollar and a million dollars have exactly the same energy. So why do you think it is so difficult to have a million dollars if you already have a dollar?

Energy follows thought and intention. If you want to bring something into your experience, all you have to do is invite its energy. Let me put it this way: before you had a physical body, all you were was energy. Your body is created or incarnated based on energy. The same is with anything else that exists in a material form. Let's assume you want a new car. To have the car, first you must "call forth" its energy. With your attention you create it into your experience. Some call this "the law of attraction" it mainly focuses on attracting forth the energy, so that it eventually transforms into the physical reality.

There are several ways to attract the energy of anything that you desire. What you must understand first however, is that all is energy and your thoughts, words and acts create and summon that energy.

Ways to attract energy:

1. **Words**. You can speak what you want into your life. You can do this by talking about it, describing it to someone else, affirming (see chapter 22) or even discussing it as if it was there. This way, you invoke its energy to join you in the present moment.

2. **Visualization**. Imagination is a way of using your thoughts and attention to attract anything you want into your life. The concept is that you imagine the desirable event as if it is already present with you. For visualization techniques go to chapter 23.

3. **Images**. Simply by looking at the image of what you want, your awareness brings it your present moment. Some people even create vision boards and put pictures of what they want somewhere to look at every day.

4. **Thought**. All you have to do is think about it as if it has already been achieved. Your intention summons it in your present moment.

5. **Belief**. If you believe something is already yours, then it is already yours and not even the universe can deny it.

Some people find it difficult to bring what they desire into their physical reality. There are several reasons why that is. Firstly, let me explain the process of a desire before it becomes material. You decide what you want, so you attract it with any of the ways mentioned above. When you have created enough momentum, or in other words, when there is enough energy the desire is strong and dominant and ready to materialize. Then it waits for the opportunity to be able to manifest into your physical reality. If you are ready for it, if you believe it can happen or that it is already done, you go with the flow, allowing the opportunities to guide you to it.

REASONS THAT THE LAW OF ATTRACTION MIGHT NOT WORK:

1. Some people have difficulty it is because they want it too much. If you want it too much then it means you believe you do not have it yet. In other words you notice that it isn't there with you, so they contradict its energy and you do not allow it to become physical.

2. Another reason is that you become stuck in the attracting process. By asking for it over and over, and trying to attract it, you do not allow yourself to be guided to the moment where it will become reality.

3. Some of you might even stress on how it will come or when, don't do that, it will find its way and at a time when you, and all involved, are ready to receive it.

4. Perhaps you give up, or you become frustrated and angry, maybe you don't believe it can happen. All these are blocking the energy of a desire.

- There is a thorough explanation of the law of attraction and how it works on the book "The truth of all that is" as it comes from the Angels' perspective.

- Once you attract the energy of anything, it becomes linked with you until it finally manifests.

- It doesn't take too long for the desire to charge and enter your life. A few times of attention is all that it needs.

- The better way to allow a desire to is to let it go. Believe it will happen someday, somehow and allow it to come on its own.

22. HOW TO USE AFFIRMATIONS

Affirmation is a repeated phrase or sentence used to "enter" that information onto your subconscious. When it is implemented into the subconscious, then it becomes a belief and it is manifested in our physical experience easily.

Based on the "law of attraction" whatever is a belief, it is attracted in our experience. Usually however, we perceive reality as it is. If we want something and we don't have it, we assume it is not there. The belief that it is not there, is implemented in our subconscious and we don't allow the energy of what we want to manifest in our physical reality. With affirmations, we rewrite sentences so that we believe them and therefore, allow them in our physical experience.

Moreover, affirmations work best, because they rewrite any negative beliefs from the subconscious to make our life easier. If one believes that money comes hard, then they do not allow the wealth energy to enter their experience. The same goes with health, if a dominant belief is that a disease can't heal or at least not easily, then you continue with the same way not allowing to heal. The natural way of the universe is abundant; the natural state of our body is health. If you implement it in your subconscious then you will stop contradicting the natural flow of the energy.

The good news is that affirmations are very easy to use; however, they need a lot of repetition. Once you decide the affirmation or affirmations you want to implement into your subconscious follow the methods below.

Ways to use affirmations:

1. Create an affirmation that is positive, and in the first person subject. For instance "I am always healthy and full of energy."

2. Repeat this affirmation as often as you can, especially in the morning, and before you drift to sleep. You can either write an affirmation, or speak it out loud. In any way that you choose, do it consciously and pay attention to the feeling that it comes right after you affirm. Usually, when you believe what are affirming, you instantly feel at ease and more joyful. If you don't believe it yet, repetition is the key. Every time you affirm, you will be closer to believing it. Once you believe it, it is implemented onto your subconscious and becomes a reality.

3. Do not contradict your affirmation. When you go affirm it regularly and they you complaint about how things are (in reality) then you rewrite the affirmation from your subconscious.

Let me give you an example. You have been affirming "Money always comes easily to me." Then you complain "I don't have enough money, I'm tired, it is difficult to earn money." Then all the work you have been doing is for nothing. So next time you complain don't, instead, affirm.

Powerful affirmations:

I have created some affirmations for you to help you. Go through the list and choose the ones that make you feel better.

- Money is flowing to me easily and effortlessly.

- I have money to spent, provide for others, cover my needs, and still I have plenty to save.

- My savings account is getting bigger and bigger.

- I am wealthy, healthy and loved.

- My life is filled with people who love and appreciate me.

- I have the perfect companion that completes me in all levels.

- I succeed anything I set my intention to.

- Opportunities show up for me in all areas of my life.

- I love what I am doing. My job fulfills and satisfies me.

- I am highly clairvoyant and clairaudient.

- I am courageous and I stand up for myself.

- I am surrounded by abundance, love, and joy.

- The universe brings me what I truly desire.

- I deserve the best life and I get it.

- I radiate beauty, charisma, and grace.

- My body is shaped according to my desires.

- I am a Divine being that gives and receives good.

- My body and mind are getting healthier and stronger each day.

- I accept and I love all that I am.

- The right people find their way to me, to inspire, assist and strengthen me.

- I have the perfect family, loving, healthy, and inspiring.

- My business is growing, expanding, and thriving.

- I let go of anything that is not serving me and detoxify thoughts, people and beliefs so that I am only surrounded by beauty, love and support.

- The warmth of love surrounds me.

- The right person that loves me unconditionally and completes me has arrived.

23. HOW TO VISUALIZE

The method of visualization is used to attract desirable events into your physical experience. It uses imagination to imprint a belief into our subconscious that something is already in our possession.

As the subconscious believes it, it does no longer contradict it and so it allows us to follow the opportunities that will lead us to its materialization. Visualization can also be used as a way to ask for what we want, so we can attract its energy. Both way, this technique is powerful and as with anything, the more you use it, the better we get at it.

There are mainly two ways to use visualization: while in meditation, usually following some guided meditation to help create the images; or consciously with your own imagination.

When you have a clear desire of what you want to attract into your life, follow the steps below.

Steps to visualization:

1. Choose a scene that represents the desire you want to attract. For instance if you want a raise, picture yourself holding the new paycheck. If you want a new car, imagine you are driving it, if you want a great partner, picture yourself on a date. Find a scene that makes you feel happy as if what you want is already in your life.

2. Recreate the events of that scene, with all your senses. Make it as vivid as possible and add any details such as smells, sounds, places, and people. Be as detailed as you can and try to achieve an intense emotion. Make is as realistic as you can and recreate the image for more than five minutes.

3. Repeat the visualization technique every day, or until you feel you have accomplished its purpose. You will know by the feeling it brings out to you. If you get excitement, appreciation, euphoria then it has been successful. The effects of a successful visualization will be really dominant in your life as well, as you will be happier, and more positive.

It is really fun and you should do it just to feel good, and have fun. Do not stress to make this scene happen or set a schedule to do it several times a day because then you will be trying too hard. If you struggle, then you are creating the opposite effect.

24. HOW TO MAXIMAZE YOUR POSITIVE ATTRACTIVE ENERGY

This chapter is useful for those who try to attract a desirable event into their lives using the "law of attraction" (chapter 21). As discussed in previous chapter, few ways to attract anything is to think of it, visualize or affirm it. However, if your energy is low the energy you attract is limited. In this chapter I bring you a few simple, yet effective ways you can maximize your positive attractive energy. This chapter can also be seen as an extension of "how to raise your vibration" in chapter 5, as the following ways help to raise your overall energy.

The higher your energy, the more attraction you emit for anything you desire. This chapter is called "how to maximize your attractive energy" because consciously or unconsciously you easily become a grand manifestator of anything you put your attention into, wanted or unwanted.

The following methods should become your way of life. If you get used to applying them, your life will magically change. Do not think of them as tasks. Add them in your schedule, and eventually you would not be able to do without them. The next three ways, will not only help you to maximize your attractive energy and raise your vibration, but also they make you a happier and healthier person.

Ways to maximize your attractive energy, raise your vibration, and bring well-being into your life

1. **Appreciation.** Find a way to add appreciation into your everyday life. To successfully use this technique, you must feel great gratitude. You can do this by thinking of how an experience or event was useful to you, or why you like it. This method can be used for anything, even the simplest things. A person, an event, the breeze on your skin, the music you like, the food you eat.

You can choose one or a combination of the following ways to add appreciation into your life.

a. Reprogram yourself to pause regularly through the day and feel heartfelt emotions of gratitude for anything that you experience during that day.

b. Every night think of all that happened during the day and be as grateful as you can for all them, naming why you are grateful for each one.

c. Keep a gratitude diary. Writing is more effective than thinking. I suggest you keep a diary and write down daily, or even have it with you, and write down anything you spot something that you are grateful for.

d. Whenever you appreciate something in your life, say thank you and mean it. Praise a job well done, or even praise nature for something beautiful you spotted. If you liked the work you did, say bravo to yourself.

2. Be present. We live life passively most of the times, we do not really acknowledge what is happening around us, but we only focus on what we are doing at each moment and ignore the rest. The truth is this is not living life at the fullest. Change that, program yourself to pause regularly to notice all that is happening around you.

Let me guide you through my present right now, just to help you get the hang on this. Right now I notice the quiet, I appreciate it. I notice the comfort of my sit, I notice the temperature in the room and how it is perfect. I notice the cats sleeping next to me, I enjoy their company. I notice the room and I like the warmth that it brings me.

Now it is your turn, notice everything that exists around you and appreciate them now.

3. Positive expectations. Positive emotions have high energy. If you expect something wonderful to happen, you allow room for wonderful things to enter your life. On the contrary, if you complain, you disallow them.

Everyday state *"something wonderful is going to happen today"*. If you begin something state "this is going to turn out wonderfully". You may include this in your everyday routine, before you cook a meal, before you go for a visit and so forth. State how you want it to turn out and voila, your wish is the universe's command.

25. HOW TO FORGIVE AND CLEAR YOUR KARMA

Clearing your karma is like cleansing your soul from wrong repeated patterns. Those patterns follow you through your lifetimes until you finally clear them. Those patterns might be mistakes that you keep repeating, or people that you can't forgive. They keep reoccurring until you accept and work through them. The way to do that is to recognize them and decide to release them. In this chapter I guide you through the releasing process; however, to successfully clear them you have to make an effort to forgive yourself and others.

A karmic pattern repeats not as a punishment, but as a learning standpoint. The belief that whatever you saw you shall reap, it is quite valid, but as a way to understand what you have caused and to learn from it so as to not repeat it again. A karmic pattern is released once you stop repeating it.

Let me give you an example of karmic pattern. If you have an argument in one life time with a person that you turned to despite, that emotion needs to be cleared. If you don't forgive that person, he /she is going to show up in your next lifetime with an event that will cause you the same emotion, to cause you to deal with it. If you don't forgive them, but you keep adding to that emotion, then this karmic pattern is going to be repeated again in another life with that person being as close to you as a child or a parent and making this attempt even more difficult. It occurs even more intense in this way, to help you deal and release it so you break free. The same patterns will repeat with any mistakes that you make until you finally make the right, healthy choices.

To begin with, this chapter focuses on relationships. You shouldn't hold resentment towards another, because it will cause you unhappiness and it is going to be repeated again in more lives. Understand that this is a process that must be dialed with, and it requires determination and willpower on your behalf. Forgiving is the right thing to do, for you and for them, as you will release unhealthy behavior that causes negative patterns and limitations.

If you want to be free and release any karmic patterns, you have to first acknowledge those relationships. Find any unhealthy relationships by any strong negative emotions towards others. You might hold resentment, hate, jealousy, disappointment, anger or any other negative emotion towards them. If you do, the stronger that negative emotion, are the ones that need to be dialed with first.

When you are ready to begin follow the steps below. Try the technique with one person at a time.

STEPS TO FORGIVE AND CLEAR KARMIC PATTERNS WITH OTHERS

1. Hold the intention of forgiving that person, and forgive yourself.

2. Pray to Archangel Zadkiel. This Archangel comes to help to smooth any resentment and hate you have towards others. Invoke him with a prayer:

> *"Archangel Zadkiel, please help me clear toxic energy from my consciousness. Help me be at peace and have compassion with myself. Help me to forgive _____ from what has been done and said in this and in any other lifetimes. Thank you Archangel Zadkiel."*

3. Find a picture of the person and as you look at it, think of what has made you so upset with them in this lifetime. Speak to the person as if they were there and tell them all that have upset you.

4. Try to see the other person's point of view in this situation, not pointing fingers, but try to understand and accept the reason and emotion that made them act in a certain way.

5. At another time, take the picture again and try to find things that you like in that person. This might be anything from physical appearance to character traits, manners, behavior.

6. Repeat step 3, and then step 1. Are your emotions toward that person milder? Is anger or resentment towards them more distant? Repeat all steps again until you notice any negative emotions vanish away.

7. Forgive. Once resentment and anger vanish, all you have to do is forgive. Look at the picture again, and go through steps 1 and 2. Ultimately tell them that you are ready to release this negative pattern, and to free both of you from any negative karma. Say:

> *"I forgive you for now, and for the past, and I release any negative patterns between us into the light. We are now both free to begin again. I forgive you, and thank you that you have made me stronger."*

If you are not yet ready to forgive, I suggest you try some guided meditations on forgiveness.

PART 2:

ADVANCED SPIRITUALISTS

26. HOW TO DEVELOP YOUR INTUITION

Your intuition helps you to understand messages from spirit. It guides you to make the right choices; it is the voice of your higher power. Enhancing your intuition is the most important part to find your path.

Intuition is a feeling or belief about certain things. It is associated with the known "gut feeling". You may not know how you receive certain information, yet you feel you know the answer. Even if it is about a person, a psychic reading, an opportunity that lies ahead, your higher-self guides you from within through your intuition.

There are several ways that intuition helps us through the day. It helps to make healthy choices and to know if any person, action or opportunity is beneficial. It brings messages from our higher self, warnings and guidance, it helps us to understand and communicate with spirit, either clairaudiently, clairvoyantly, or with using any divination tools. The gift of intuition is necessary to understand divine guidance.

There are a few ways that might help you develop your intuition, but it is not a skill that can be mastered in a few attempts. The more you skill your intuition, the better it gets.

Ways to develop your intuition

1. **Trust what you receive**. A way to develop your intuition is to get rid of uncertainty. You may get it wrong some times, but if you believe that you make the right choices, then your belief in your intuition gets stronger, and you rely on it with confidence. This is also the key, to develop it. Trust what comes from within, the more you do, the stronger the knowing gets.

2. **Guessing games**. Everyone loves games, and there are plenty you can do to "guess" using your intuition. I give you two examples to help you get started.

- Have someone pick a number, an object, a card or anything that you will have to guess. Close your eyes and silently ask your higher self to direct you to the answer. Then trust the answer that comes. You will get a thought pop in your mind, or perhaps an image. It might be really mild, but go with it and see what comes of it.

- Get a magazine and ask yourself what exists in a random page number. Ask your higher self to reveal the answer through your intuition.

3. **Divination tools**. If you are new to any divination tools such as Angel cards, pendulum dowsing, you will not know what messages they bring, and rely on others or booklets to help you. With practice however, you will no longer need any direction booklets or assistance to help you understand the messages. The more you practice, the more you will understand and trust your own intuition for their interpretation.

4. People reading. Use the technique of chapter 48 to help you develop your intuition while reading the energy of others.

If you trust your intuition the stronger it gets, but the opposite is also true. The less you trust it, the less develop it is.

27. HOW TO SEE AURAS

Everything that exists is made of energy. This energy surrounds the physical body but it is invisible to the untrained eye. According to the power, mood and health of each body, the energy changes color. Our body is surrounded by such energy, and many know it as "aura".

Our aura is invisible energy that is in close communication with our higher self. This energy is otherwise known as our spiritual body. Trees and animals also have an aura. Angels and spiritual beings have an energetic form too, but it is different from ours. There is a chapter to train your eyes on Angelic presence, (see chapter 46) to notice how different their colors are from our own. For this chapter however, I will help you recognize the auras of physical bodies such as people, animals and plants.

Seeing one's aura is quite useful because you recognize if they are happy, sad or have low energy. Most of all, seeing one's aura directs healers in that part of the body that needs healing. If people are in pain, then that part of your body has darker energy. A trained healer can perceive the problem instantly by seeing one's aura.

If you are not a healer, you might still find this technique interesting, as different personalities result in different colors in auras. Also the width of an aura signifies their alignment. Most adults have an aura about 2 feet (60 cm) wide. Some more spiritually- evolved or strong personalities have auras that are 5-6 feet (1.5 meters) wide.

Before I guide you through some simple steps to begin your aura recognition practice, I present some aura colors and their significance.

AURA COLORS AND THEIR SIGNIFICANCE

White: energy. At first the only color you will be able to perceive is white. This signifies the existence of energy.

Green: physical bodies that are more connected to earth, have green as part of their aura color. Animals and plants also have a green color in their aura. This means a balanced energy flow.

Blue: intelligence, high spirit, psychic ability, a spiritual person.

Yellow: logic, spontaneous, active.

Orange: playful, child-like, care-free.

Red: sexuality, procreation, pregnancy, passion. It may also signify anger when in combination with darker colors.

Brown: sickness, weakness.

Purple: spirituality, wisdom, maturity, psychic ability.

Turquoise: peace, creativity, young soul.

Gold: oneness

Grey/black: sickness, negative energy, negative thoughts.

STEPS TO SEE AURAS:

1. Hold the intention to see auras and their colors.

2. Ask for spiritual assistance to help you resolve any blockages that may prevent your clairvoyant abilities.

> *"I ask for Archangel Michael, please release me from any blockages, so that I can see the beautiful colors of energy on auras. Thank you! My powerful spiritual team of Angels and guides, I ask that you assist me to see the auras clearly through my eyes. Thank you, and so it is."*

3. To begin with, find a living plant, or even better, a person. Since the colors of the aura are transparent, it helps when the background is white. Place the plant, a person willing to help you, or even your own hand, in front of a white surface or wall.

4. Focus on the person, or living plant in front of you. Try to connect with it.

5. Focus your attention around 2, 3 cm from the person, where the aura exists. Focus on one spot. Relax, let go of any thoughts or expectations and try to establish a connection. Usually, you will be able to notice a transparent line that surrounds the physical body. Focus on it, and with practice, you will be able to see its details.

- Do not worry if you can't differentiate any colors or energy yet, usually this method needs practice.

- The more you try to see auras, the more skilled you become.

- At first you will only be able to see a transparent line that shows where the aura ends. Later the aura will fill with transparent white

28. HOW TO USE PENDULUM DAWSING

There are various divination techniques that work as a mediator translating energy from spirit. Not all divination techniques work the same way, or match your own energy. You may find one divination technique difficult and inaccurate for instance, while you may love another. Experiment, is the way to find which one you love the most.

Pendulum dowsing is a very easy technique and anyone can do it.

It consists of any kind of small object that you hold at the end side of a string. Some people use crystals, as it allows energy to direct it, while others use light materials such, a cross or a necklace. Pendulum dowsing is the technique of asking yes or no questions and spirit or your own higher self, responds through it by moving in patterns to answer your question.

As a child, and even now, I am fascinated with the way a pendulum moves on its own, without any external force directing it. It is a confirmation for forces outside of our physical reality.

Pendulum works by translating the vibrations of spirit into motions that you have chosen beforehand. It usually works with your own higher self that knows all the answers already, and interprets the vibration from your hand to the string, that then translates it as movement.

When you have a pendulum and some questions in mind, follow the steps that follow.

STEPS TO PENDULUM DAWSING:

1. **Protection**. As used in any other technique. Call me over-protective, but I always go through a shielding process. Pick one from chapter 4.

2. **Clear your pendulum.** If your pendulum is a crystal, you should go through a crystal clearing process first (see chapter 3).

Hold your pendulum and ask it to be cleared. I usually ask Archangel Michael to assist me with this step.

> *"Archangel Michael of the light, I call upon you now, to cleanse and clear any negative energies or interferences from this pendulum, so that it is only brings accurate answers. Thank you, and so it is."*

3. **Direct the pendulum.** This step is important, if your pendulum is a crystal. Hold your pendulum and direct it, assign it a task. It is important for a crystal to be programmed so it knows who it belongs to, and how it can serve. Here is an example:

> *"You are my pendulum, used for dowsing to bring me accurate responses to my questions. You should only work with lighted beings that work for the highest good of all. It is my intention that you assist me in that way, thank you, and so it is."*

Some people might not think this step is important; however I always go through this process for all my crystals.

4. Program it. You should now assign it the movements that it will use to respond. You can make up the movements you want to assign it, however I give you an example with the most common ones.

Make the pendulum move up and down and then say: "This is for yes." Pause, stop the pendulum's movement and then ask it. "Please, show me a yes." Naturally, the pendulum will move on its own showing you a clear up and down movement, meaning yes. If it doesn't repeat the process until it shows you a clear yes movement.

Direct the pendulum's movement towards left and right. Then say: "This is for no." Pause, stop the pendulum's movement and then ask it. "Please, show me a no."

You can assign it more movements, as long as they are clear to you and you will not confuse them with any others you have previously assigned. You might use the circular movement as a "maybe" or "possibly" or "don't know".

5. Invoke spirit assistance. Ask for your higher self, or your spirit guides and Angels to be present and help you find answers through the pendulum. Do this so you avoid any unnecessary curious spirits interfering.

> *"I call upon my highest and most helpful guides, please be present with me and help me get accurate and valid responses from this pendulum. Thank you for your kind assistance."*

6. Ask. Now all that is left is to get guidance. Ask the pendulum precise yes/no questions that you are ready to know the answer to. Don't ask something that you only want the pendulum to show yes for instance. Does he love me? If you are not ready to accept either response, the pendulum response will not be accurate. This is because your own thoughts and desires interfere with the movement, and secondly because your guides do not want to upset you.

- The lighter the pendulum, the easier it is to move. Do not go for a bigger crystal, but something smaller is better.

- The string of the pendulum shouldn't be long to interpret the answers more easily.

- When you are dowsing, do not rest your elbow, as it stops the energy from entering the string.

- You cannot know with accuracy anything that did not happen yet. Do not expect it to guide you to lottery numbers or future facts because the future is yet unknown even to your guides.

29. HOW TO USE ANGEL CARDS

Angel cards are much similar to tarot cards. However, unlike the tarot cards the messages are very soothing and loving. They never bring any negative messages. Due to their high frequency and kind messages, they attract lighted beings that bring you messages through them.

If you have ever wondered if Angel cards or tarot cards work as divination tools, the answer is yes. As you focus on a question, spirits follow your thoughts that reply with the right cards. There is a process that needs to be followed for an accurate reading. The trick is being guided to choose the right cards and then trusting your intuition to interpret them. Spirit directs the energy of the cards so that the appropriate card may fall off the deck, strike your attention, or even guide your movements to pick the suited ones.

For interpreting the cards, there is a standard booklet for any card you choose, which guides you through the answers; however, spirit directs the interpretation of each card through intuition as well. The more skilled you become, the more you understand the meaning of the cards without needing any instruction booklet to help you.

I was fascinated with this method of divination from my teen years. I loved to ask a question and then find out what the cards were telling me. Of course, most of the time the messages didn't make sense, they were confusing and did not apply to my situation. This is because I didn't know how to prepare the cards and myself in order to be guided to the right answers. I did not rely in my intuition, yet I was in awe of those who didn't need any booklet but yet gave the best personalized readings. Thinking of this now makes me realize how much I have learned. The cards work as divination tools and you are the right interpreter. To develop your intuition, see chapter 26.

You can use Angel cards or tarot cards to answer your own questions, get guidance, or assist someone else by using the cards.

Choosing a deck of cards is similar to choosing a crystal. Sense the energy of each deck, observe its colors and images to discover the one that you love. Each deck brings different messages that will help you each time. Trust your intuition for this step as well.

When you have your deck, let's begin.

STEPS TO USE ANGEL CARDS OR TAROT CARDS:

1. Find a quiet place where you won't have any distractions.

2. Cleanse your cards. Your cards may hold negative energy that makes them "heavy" and confuse you when choosing the right card for a reading. There are several ways you can cleanse your cards.

a. Invoke Archangel Michael.

"I ask for the loving Archangel Michael, please step forth and join me now. please cleanse my cards, and remove any negative energy so that they only bring me accurate answers to my questions. Thank you, and so it is."

b. Tap the cards twice, and imagine that any negative energy that they hold, drops and dissolves.

c. Hold the cards. In your mind ask that they are completely cleansed. Imagine white, cleansing light surrounding you and the cards.

d. Crystal cleansing. You can place a cleansing crystal on the deck for a few hours. The crystal will absorb any negative energy. Crystals that are appropriate for this are:

3. Invite Angels and lighted beings to help you with the reading.

"I call upon lighted Angels to bring me accurate answers through these cards. Please guide my hands to pick the right cards, guide my thoughts to give accurate interpretations. Guide me what I should know. Thank you, thank you, thank you."

4. Ask a question. As you shuffle the cards ask them a question. The more specific question, the more appropriate will be the answer. Remember, the future is yet unknown, or there are multiple possibilities, so avoid asking any questions about the future.

5. Choose the right cards. There are several ways you can do this.

When you ask your question and a card falls off the deck, you better choose that card as there is a reason it fell off the deck.

a. You can spread the cards in front of you and follow your gaze. You are guided towards the right card with your eyes. Usually a card gets your attention more than others. Pick that one.

b. You can shuffle, cut the deck in half, and pick the firsts cards in the order they appear.

c. You can close your eyes and follow your hands as they choose the right cards from the pile.

6. Spread your cards. There are several ways you can position the cards. Each one may bring you an extra message in a certain position. You can find card spreads in your deck's booklet. Or you can make up your own spread.

I usually choose 9 cards and place them 3x3 without paying any extra attention to their position. When I am confused about a card and what it represents, I pick another card from the deck and combine their messages.

7. Interpret the cards. You can either choose the deck's booklet to help you with the interpretations or you can trust your intuition about what each card means.

Remember to be open to any answers you receive.

8. Thank the Angels for assisting you with the reading.

You can even make your own deck. You can print some images online and assign your own interpretations.

30. HOW TO REMOVE BLOCKAGES

Any negative believes sabotage the perfect flow of energy; they are called blockages. They exist in your subconscious and they are added through various instances in your lives. You may have absorbed them growing up, create them due to fear or insecurities; or you may have observed them in others. Blockages are usually created due to repetition and for this you cannot release them so easily; they are imprinted in your subconscious.

Such negative believes may exist in several areas of your life, and prevent you from allowing beneficial opportunities in your life. Some examples of blockages is the belief that money comes hard, that you need to struggle to thrive, that you are not beautiful, that others' opinions matter more than yours, that you are likely to fail, or even that economy is bad. Those are only some examples of negative beliefs that may be general or specific to you. Those beliefs might prevent you from abundance, health and good opportunities for growth and expansion.

In my previous book "The truth of all that is" the Angels explain about blockages and how you can remove them. If you didn't yet read that book, I will summarize the processes in the following steps.

HOW TO REMOVE BLOCKAGES OR LIMITING BELIEFS

1. Identify negative beliefs.

   a. Sit and contemplate upon any negative beliefs you may have. Write them all down.

   b. Scratch that negative statement of your page and replace it with a matching positive one.

   c. Call upon Angels for assistance to help you release the negative patterns and replace them with the new ones.

   "I call upon the most loving Angels that can most assist me at this time, please come and detoxify me from limiting beliefs, help me to erase them from my subconscious mind and from my life now and forever. Help me make way for the opportunities to flow to me through positive empowering thoughts. I am ready to release the old ones and replace them with the new. Thank you , thank you, thank you, and so it is."

2. Be aware of your thoughts and words at any time. Stop yourself before speaking or thinking any negative statements. Instead replace them with the opposite positive statements. Here is an example: "I don't have enough money for what I want to buy." Replace: "I am always provided for, and I have enough for all my needs, and desires." Even if you don't believe it, in time, the false statement will be replaced in your subconscious. When it does, the universe immediately takes effect treasuring you with opportunities of abundance."

- Be patient and determined to release any limiting beliefs. The key is to be aware of your thoughts and words at any time.

31. HOW TO DELETE HEART VOWS

Through many of our lifetimes, we have experienced some hardships and struggles that caused us to make vows, promises or contracts to protect ourselves. These vows become locked in our Akashic records and repeat over and over for each lifetime.

You may have difficulty with money for instance; did it ever occur to you that the source of this goes back lifetimes? You may have sworn never to have money again as you thought it was the source of evil or hardship. Many people have taken this vow, and it is called **vow of poverty**.

Silence vows, may have begun from a past lifetime when you were a monk and sworn to be silent. The effects may be evident today, as you may find it difficult to speak your mind.

Imperfection vows. This may sound silly to you, but some souls prefer to mask their beauty in different ways such as extra weight you find extremely hard to get rid of, unclean skin, or any other way that masks your beauty. Some people were misused and raped in the past because of their pretty. They caused that their "curse" and wished they weren't pretty.

Love vows. When someone was deeply hurt, thee may make vows not to love again.

Lonliness vows. Swearing to live in solitarily to find peace, or be close to God.

Suffering. Some religions believed and still believe that suffering is a way to purify the soul. This absolutely does not stand.

Sacrifice. Giving up everything to balance the karma for something they have done, or to prove their wholeness to god.

Marriage. These vows link you with the other soul through many lifetimes, that you keep repeating and you end up marring the same person, even if you don't know it. The clearest sign of vows spoken is "for better or worse until death do as apart". Since death is only temporary, when there is life, the vow repeats.

There may other vows that you have done through many lifetimes, but the ones mentioned above are the most common. Releasing them and breaking those vows will help you to be free and start again without anything holding you causing you to make the same mistakes.

The good news is breaking such vows, it is as easy as creating them.

WAYS TO RELEASE HEART VOWS:

1. Work with the Angels: The Angels assist us anytime we need them. Simply invoke them and ask them with the following words:

"I call upon my guardian Angels, spirit guides, and the Akashic record keepers. I lovingly ask you to release me from any vows, promises or contracts I have made in this or any other lifetime. Please cancel, clear and delete them from all dimensions of time. Thank you, thank you, thank you."

2. Cancel vows verbally, the same way you have created them. Repeat three times.

"I rescind and withdraw all vows, deeds, covenants, and promises in this and all lifetimes, in all realms and dimensions and in all time and space. So be it."

-     Be careful not to rewrite such vows as your thoughts and words never go unnoticed.

32. HOW TO ATTRACT WEALTH

Since you are reading this chapter now, you are ready to welcome financial abundance into your life. You need to understand that wealth is energy. If you want to attract prosperity do not think of it as a material thing, but as energy.

You have to be keen towards the energy of abundance as you welcome it daily in your life through your thoughts and actions. If you speak or think lack of money, you limit the energy of wealth from your experience. On the other hand, if you think prosperous thoughts and give share you have a lot, then you summon forth wealth.

In this chapter I am going to suggest various techniques and exercises that will help you to allow the flow of wealth into your experience.

The Angels say: "How many times we tell you that it is very easy to attract wealth, you block it due to your current circumstances, and believe that money comes by with difficulty." Few people don't have this belief, and they are those who are wealthy. They have accepted that money comes and goes. As money follows energy and thought, wealth follows those with wealthy mindset. Similarly, ANYONE can be wealthy. The same energy is needed to summon forth a penny and a billion dollars. The problem with this image is that you think that it is easy to find a penny, but you believe it is extremely hard or unlikely for you to get a billion dollars. This is when you block the energy of billion dollars. The energy of both amounts is there, but your belief either summons or detracts it.

Having said all these, let's work on some exercises to help you attract the energy of abundance. First step for all those methods is to remove any limiting believes regarding money. (See chapter 30 on removing limiting believes). It is a good idea to release any vows of poverty as described in chapter 31.

WAYS TO ATTRACT WEALTH

1. **Summon it.** Summon the energy of wealth to enter you physical experience.

To help you do this I have created a guided meditation. Find it here: http://bit.ly/24qLSRq

a. Consider how much money you want and what you will do with that money.

b. Believe that it is done and that you will get all the money you have asked for when you are ready.

c. In a meditative state see the glowing energy of money being summoned forth and entering your aura.

The energy the money you want has now entered your Etheric form and awaits for the best opportunity to join you in your physical experience.

d. Be guided by your intuition and follow your gut. Someone, something, somehow is going to be that opportunity that will allow the money to flow in your experience. Do not doubt yourself, or the universe. Accept that money is now yours. Yes it is as easy as that.

2. Visualization. Sometimes, the best way to allow money to flow in your experience is to feel them there.

a. close your eyes and see yourself spending the money. Add as much detail as you can. See chapter 23 on visualization.

b. Repeat whenever you begin to doubt or feel lack of money.

3. Mantra. There are some mantras that attract the energy of money to your physical experience. They are quite powerful. See chapter 17 on how to use mantras.

a. "Om Sarvabaadhaa Vinirmukto, Dhan Dhaanyah Sutaanvitah, Manushyo Matprasaaden Bhavishyati Na Sanshayah Om"

b. "Om Shring Shriye Namah"

c. Shreem

d. "Om Shree Mahalakshmyai Cha Vidraahe Vishnu Patrayai Cha Dheemahi Tanno Lakshmi Prachodayat Om"

e. "Om Shreem Maha Lakshmiyei Namaha"

4. Archangel Ariel. This loving Archangel helps you to summon and allow financial wealth in your experience. Invoke Archangel Ariel with this prayer.

> *"I call forth the loving Archangel Ariel and all Angels of prosperity. Please help me release any liming beliefs that prevent me from wealth. Please erase all karmic contracts that may prevent me from wealth, as well as release any limiting emotions and thoughts so that I can enjoy prosperity in this lifetime. I ask that you help me receive _____ (name how much money or what exactly you want to summon with that money) that I promise to use for good. I thank you dearly and I have hope in your power. Thank you, thank you, thank you, and so it is."*

5. **Speak, think and act as you already have all you want**. Do not think twice to give to another as money will come back to you in more ways and amounts. Speak as if you have what you want, think as if you are already wealthy. This way you direct energy that follows thoughts, words and actions.

6. **Donate**. This is a very powerful way to attract the flow of prosperity. As you give money, you allow the energy to flow in and out of your life. If you don't allow money to flow, then it gets blocked and you can't receive it either. Don't think that if you give you will not have enough, because the opposite occurs. As you give, more comes in.

Also with sharing and giving you clear your karma and strengthen your aura.

- As already mentioned, remove any limiting beliefs In order for the processes to be successful.

- Trust that it is done, and let it go. Don't repeat it as that tells the universe you don't trust it, nor your power and you doubt.

- Believe that is really easy to get all you want

- Follow your instinct. Money is not going to fall on your lap, but the universe will bring you ways to help you get them. For instance if you get an urge to speak to a person do it. If you get an idea to write a book, do it. It might lead to your prosperity.

- Universe finds abundant ways to bring forth what you want. If you miss one opportunity, another one will come along.

33. HOW TO FEEL ANGELS

Most of the times, any direct form of connection with spirit happens internally. Clairaudients receive an inner voice similar to their thoughts, clairvoyants mental images, similar to their own imagination, others with clairsentience ability receive a feeling and so on. All those ways are a link of connection between physical and spiritual. But what about actual physical evidence from spirit?

If you are like me, you prefer physical evidence of spirit, that id undeniable. Even now, I sometimes question whether I receive spirit communication or if it is my own imagination (yes it happens to all of us). This is because inner communication can easily be missed, misinterpreted, or if you don't practice enough, it is tough to distinguish.

Subsequently, I have created the following processes to be 101% certain I am not going crazy! In brief, I have asked the Angels or any lighted beings that I communicate with, to send me clear proof of their presence.

I have received the following signs from spirit: I got a few signs but the more distinct were my chandelier moving in circles every time I channeled, even if all the windows were closed. I saw lighted beams of energy near my bed at night. I received random breeze of soft air on my skin. I heard humming noises I actually caught on tape: (check them out here: http://bit.ly/1RalCjV)

And finally, I sensed physical Angelic touches. Follow the steps below to do so as well.

HOW TO FEEL ANGEL PRESENCE

1. Relax, or even better meditate just to clear your mind and de-clutter your thoughts.

2. Protect yourself (see chapter 4).

3. Release any fear and get ready to receive an Angel's touch on your skin. If have any thoughts of fear, the Angels will not make contact with you in this way, since they don't want to scare you.

4. Light a candle to create a peaceful welcoming environment. (De-clutter your space since they don't like clutter. See chapter 9.)

5. Raise your hand with the palm upwards in a comfortable position so you don't strain it. Then invite them with the following invocation. Choose any Angel that you prefer to come forth at any time, or ask for the Angel that can most assist at that time to join you.

   "I ask for _____ /the most lighted Archangel that can most assist at this time; please join me, and help me feel your energy on my raised palm. I ask that you touch my hand and help me experience your lighted energy now. Thank you, thank you, thank you. I am open, I am receptive, and so it is."

6. Keep your palm open and your eyes closed, as this helps to tune you with their frequency. Allow some time, and be receptive to anything that you may feel on your hand. Know that it is a safe place, and anything you receive comes from love.

7. Wait for a few minutes, and then thank the Angel that came. If you did not receive any physical energy, do not worry; try again at another time when you are more receptive.

- I have tried this technique several times. One time I asked for Archangel Raphael, and I felt a soft breeze on my palm that stayed there for quite a while. The second time, I asked for Archangel Michael. My hand began to open and close on its own. Like someone was grasping it and moving it for me! It was quite intense both times, and I was showered with unconditional love while at the same time my vibration was raised instantly. Before they make any sort of contact with us, they want to make sure we will receive them, and be open to their energy. For this they raise our vibration enough to be able to experience them.

- All Angels are different, and I am sure if I try this technique with more Angels, the ways their energy comes through on my hand will be different as well.

I am interested to know your experiences. Please do visit my Facebook page and let me know how you experienced spirit!

https://www.facebook.com/theAngelbook/

34. HOW TO CLEAR YOUR CHAKRAS

Chakras are the energetic connection of your physical and spiritual body. If your chakras are blocked you feel unwell and drained. When you are sick, your chakras are congested with negative energy, or they lack healthy energy to work properly. We clean them so they heal and fill us with energy and spiritual connection.

Chakras are not visible to the untrained eye. They have different colors and each one has a different function.

If you are aware of chakras, you will know the seven ones that exist on our body. The truth is that there are more chakras but they have spiritual functions. For this chapter I stand on the seven ones that lie on our physical body.

THE CHAKRAS

1. Root or Base chakra: Base of spine in tailbone area.

Color: red

Represents: existence, our alignment with the physical body and feeling of being grounded.

If this chakra is imbalanced: Anemia, fatigue, lower back pain, depression, Cold.

This chakra also affects our prosperity levels and food addictions.

2. **Sacral or sex Chakra**: Lower abdomen

Color: orange

Represents: connection with others, acceptance, feelings and empathy.

If this chakra is imbalanced: Eating disorders. Alcohol and drug problems. Depression. Low back pain. Asthma or allergies. Urinary problems. Sexual issues.

On an emotional level it affects sexuality and pleasure, well-being.

3. **Solar plexus chakra**: above the navel

Color: yellow

Represents: confidence, ego power, self-control, self-esteem.

If it is imbalanced: Digestive problems, diabetes, hypoglycemia, constipation, anxiety, and poor memory.

4. **Hearth chakra**: center of chest

Color: green

Represents: love, relationships, compassion, forgiveness, joy, inner peace.

If imbalanced: heart problems, chest pain, high blood- pressure, immune problems

5. Throat chakra: middle of throat

Color: blue

Represents: Communication, self-expression, speaking of the truth, standing up for oneself

If imbalanced: Thyroid imbalances, swollen glands, Infections, Mouth, jaw, tongue, neck and shoulders problems. Swings, and menopause.

6. Third eye chakra: Between eyebrows.

Color: indigo blue

Represents: intuition, imagination, clairvoyance, insights, inspiration.

If imbalanced: fevers, headaches

7. Crown chakra: top of the head

Color: violet

Represents: oneness, bliss, higher connection

If imbalanced: mental illness, headaches, heaviness

Ways to clear chakras:

1. **Crystal clearing:** This method cleanses and empowers your chakras. Lie down for thirty minutes and add the following crystals on top your basic chakras. There are alternatives to this chakra cleansing technique, feel free to find more information if necessary. Before you begin, cleanse your stones in the ways I mention below, and then begin the clearing process.

   a. Add a red crystal or gem like bloodstone, hematite or garnet on your base chakra (connection with earth, finance, survival) that is at the base of your spine.

   b. Add a crystal or gem like red jasper, red and brown aventurine, carnelian, orange calcite or zincite on your sacral chakra, (emotions) that is around your reproductive organs.

   c. Place a stone like yellow jasper, golden calcite, amber, topaz citrine or yellow sapphire on your solar plexus chakra, (governs self-esteem, transformation) that is situated around the navel and up to the breastbone.

   d. Place an emerald, green calcite, green tourmaline, malachite, moonstone, rose quartz, or jade on your heart chakra (relationships) that is in the center of your chest.

   e. For the fifth chakra, place a blue turquoise, aquamarine, blue topaz, blue kyanite, blue calcite or Angelite on the area of your throat chakra (speak the truth) that is on the base of your throat.

   f. Place amethyst, azurite, lapis lazuli or sodalite on your third eye chakra (mental vision, consciousness) that is between your eyebrows.

g. Finally add a quartz, diamond, clear calcite, white topaz or amethyst on your crown chakra (divinity, cosmic consciousness, spiritual wisdom) that is on the top of your head.

The crystals should be placed in a straight line on the areas mentioned above. You should then relax and experience their energy clearing for around thirty minutes.

2. Visualization

a. Lie on your back and relax.

b. Close your eyes take deep slow breaths and relax your thoughts and mind.

c. Visualize the color red at the base of your spine (base chakra) as a glowing ball of red light. Hold the intention of clearing any negative energy from that area, and empowering it with healthy vibrant light. Feel your breath moving in and out from this center while continuing to imagine a red ball of light emanating from that location. Spent a minute on this area visualizing the red light.

d. Move up to the sex chakra and repeat the exercise with the color orange for a minute, always having the intention of clearing and energizing that chakra.

e. Similarly work with the solar plexus, with the color yellow.

f. now imagine the heart chakra, filling with green glowing color.

g. The throat chakra filling and energizing with blue color.

h. The third eye chakra with indigo blue.

i. Lastly, the crown chakra with a violet color.

155

g. Once you complete the cycle, Affirm: "I am healthy, balanced and at peace.

3. Healing with the Archangel Michael and Archangel Raphael.

These two powerful Archangels usually work together to release negative energy, and then heal it from our physical bodies.

"I lovingly ask for Archangel Michael, to please cleanse and clear all my chakras, so they are realized from any negative energy. I lovingly ask for Archangel Raphael, to heal any abnormalities on my chakras and empower them with healing light. Thank you, thank you, thank you. And so it is."

Relax, or meditate, and allow a few minutes for the Archangels to work on your chakras.

35. HOW TO FIND LOST OBJECTS

How many times did you lose something and hoped you knew where it was? The truth is, you can! As you develop your intuition, you can find out anything. That is why I love being intuitive, it can really be handy.

WAYS TO FIND LOST ITEMS

1. **Intuition**. It doesn't matter if you are clairaudient, or clairvoyant, if you connect with your higher divinity, you get a glimpse of where that item might be. Similar to enhancing your intuition, (see chapter 26) you can tune into your inner power for guidance.

a. Set your intention. I want to know where _____ is.

b. Ask for Divine help.

"I lovingly call forth Archangel Chamuel. Please help me find _____ or for it to be returned to me. Thank you for your kind assistance, and so it is."

c. Ask your higher self to reveal the missing object and trust your intuition. Similar to automatic writing (see chapter ____) ask your higher self to tell or show you where the item is. Then just remove all thoughts and listen to the response. You might hear a word, see an image, or get a knowing of where it might be, trust it.

2. **Meditation.** Ask your guides to help you find the lost item while in meditation. They will reveal the answer to you.

3. **Pendulum dowsing**. Reference chapter 28 on how to work with a pendulum. When you are ready to begin, bring in your mind the image of your lost object. Then ask the pendulum questions. You can begin with: is my lost item inside? If yes, is it near me now? is it on the second floor? Is it on the floor?

You get the idea; keep going until you narrow it down.

36. HOW TO ENHANCE YOUR SPIRITUAL CONNECTION

There are days you feel aligned, you receive messages from spirit, have inspiration, and get nudges from the Ether. Those times, you are able to channel clearly, there are other times however, that you try over and over, but you don't seem to align. The good news is, it happens to the best of us. Don't beat yourself up. You can easily get your alignment and spiritual connection back.

The term alignment or spiritual connection includes any sort of channeling, inspiration or intuition you may have. If at one point you were practicing spiritual connection regularly and then you stopped, you might feel disconnected and hard to align again after a period of time. Do not worry, you can never lose your gift, it is always there but you need practice to get yourself aligned with it.

Additionally, there are times that you feel aligned and other that you don't. Usually, it has to do with your own vibration. The natural state of well-being is bliss. When you are happy you meet your higher self and the connection is strong. If you are unwell, sad, or anxious, then the gap between your physical and higher self is big and you cannot achieve spiritual connection successfully.

Imagine a week of relaxation, peace and joy. At that week, you are able to meditate every day. Let's assume you had a busy week, and couldn't meditate, clear your mind nor do something fun. In which one of the two weeks will you have a greater connection and alignment? The first one of course and that is because your vibration was raised, and your mind was clear. Thus the key to a clear communication is a raised vibration, and a relaxed mind without worries.

WAYS TO ENHANCE YOUR SPIRITUAL CONNECTION:

1. If your life is a mess, if you run through another day rushing to get things done, then your state of mind is working overtime and there is no room for anything that your higher self, or spirit might be telling you. Put your life in order. It always helps to have a calendar, as you organize your schedule, you organize your thoughts.

2. Declutter your space. Similar to your thoughts, your environment needs to be in order as well. This creates harmony and brings alignment. (See chapter 9)

3. Practice. It doesn't matter if you used to have a great spiritual connection and now you don't or whether you try to connect with spirit for the first time all that matters is practice. The more you try, the better you get at it. I recommend automatic writing. You cannot get it wrong, and the better you will get. (See chapter 40).

4. Raise your vibration for several days. (See chapter 5) return to your natural state of peace so that spirits can meet you halfway and pass on their messages and signs.

- If you used to be aligned, talk to spirit or/and receive signs, give accurate readings and then you were too busy to align, then it will not magically be "turned on" again unless you try. The more frequently you connect with spirit, the clearer the messages. This is because you get accustom to their high vibration and you can tune into their signals more easily.

37. HOW TO DEAL WITH AN UNWELCOMED SPIRIT

I want to emphasize that you may encounter unwelcomed spirits, but they are not evil. In the spirit world, there are no evil spirits, there may be troublemakers, annoying, or even lost ones, but there are no evil spirits in the sense that some think. As souls are close to source, they are pure and loving. Some may lose their way and drift from light, get confused, or even become governed by their ego side that once governed their physical body. Don't be afraid of spirits, they cannot harm you nor they intend to, but they may be unwelcomed and there are ways to get rid of them.

Most spirits are invisible to us, some might interact, and some might be passive. Certain have a reason they are there, others just play around, or get lost. You might know them as ghosts, but there are also those spirits that feel drawn to you, or are connected with you from past lives. Spirits are rarely visible to us, we might feel a presence in the room, see a shadow, hear noises, feel nudges or pokes, or even have things misplaced or knocked down. Spirits might do all those to get our attention, to show their frustration or displeasure at something, usually for their own death.

They might feel attach to a place, an object or a person. Moreover, they might deny their own death and believe they are still alive. Below, I present some of the reasons spirits still linger in our physical world.

REASONS SPIRITS LINGER ON EARTH

1. **They visit a loved one**. These spirits come to visit to get their presence known to their living relatives. They don't want to harm nor scare, but soothe and assist. If a spirit loves you so much, he/she visits years after their passing and they try to bring a message to you, or look after you. If you feel them there, and you are not comfortable with their presence, you can just ask them nicely to go on their way.

2. **Confused souls**. Some may call these ghosts. They have an attachment with the physical world that keeps them from moving on. They may be scared of judgment, grieve for their lost life, enjoy their old ways and consequently refuse to return. They may even be unaware they are dead and just live in their own imaginary world. These souls may get annoyed by the living, especially if they interact with their environment. They can never harm the living, but scare nonetheless.

3. **Past life connections.** Spirits don't know if you are in a completely different body, they are connected with your soul, and they can find you easily through time. This is especially so if you are sensitive, or you practice channeling spirit. It is like you open up the source of connection and they come through either to be with you, or show their displeasure at some wrong past life choices. These spirits get attached to your aura. These can be both positive connections, and karmic ones. In either case, they drain your energy and need to be separated.

4. For entertainment purposes. Earth is like a spirit playground. Spirits visit often to play with nature, animals, the ocean, or even us. Spirits are gentle and careful not to scare us. These sort of spirits are welcomed and not a reason to worry, or even go through the trouble of sending them away. They leave when they have their fun for a while. When I say fun, I mean that those spirits enjoy recreating their physical experiences in the places they once lived, or try to enjoy a physical experience. of course if a spirit is bothering you in any way, you can send them away.

WAYS TO DEAL WITH AN UNWELCOMED SPIRIT

1. **Ask them to leave**. All spirits can hear you, and understand you. Do it in a loving way, and encourage them to move on. For earthbound spirits or ghosts, reassure them that it is the right thing to do, and that no one will judge them in the spirit world. They will be loved and celebrated, and they should hurry on to continue their expansion.

Some of the earthbound spirits don't see the light. Help them to find it, ask them to call for their guardian Angel or spirit guide and they will help them.

2. **Archangel Michael**. This powerful Archangel can remove any earthbound spirits, or spirit connections.

> *"Loving Archangel Michael, I call upon you now. Please release me from any spirits that may be attached to me. Please assist any earthbound spirits in this house to cross over to the light. Please clear any spirits from my aura and from my home now. thank you, and so it is."*

3. **Sage**. Burning sage is a way of cleansing from any negative energies and spirits. Burn sage for yourself and your home.

4. **Intention**. Hold the intention that all spirits, or spirit attachments be released from your energy, and environment. Visualize a bright white light, cleansing yourself and your home from any spirits. Imagine any energies being released out onto the window or door and into the light.

5. **Higher self-intervention.** For spirit attachments it usually helps to ask for your higher self to intervene through the Akashic records, and release any attachments. In a relaxed state say the following out loud.

> *"I ask Divine Spirit to cut all bonds and ties between any negative karmic spirit attachments that we have, and to fully and totally release us from them completely and forever. I ask that this process begins now and continues until it is fully complete, with the assistance of the lighted Archangel Michael. Thank you, and so it is."*

For stubborn spirits, you may need to try a combination of the methods above.

38. HOW TO CUT NEGATIVE CORDS OF ATTACHMENT

As you go through your day, each item, person, place or idea you interact with, creates a connection cord with you. These cords transmit energies and emotions from one another and affect our state and well-being.

How many times did you think of a person and the phone rang with them on the other line? Or might speak about them and then they appear later that day. These are obvious signs of connection cords. They transmit signals and affect our thoughts and emotions.

When you cut a cord, you don't remove any memories, or any interactions with the person, you only cut the energy transmissions with it. This is important for people close to us as well, because if they feel down, tired or sick, they can affect our own energy and mood. The stronger the bond, the stronger the connection, and hence, the stronger the impact they have on us. I am sure you have heard of twins and how they sense one another, or they know when the other is been hurt. This is because their cords of connection are extremely strong from the constant 9 month interaction during pregnancy.

If a person has negative thoughts or emotions towards you, the cord becomes a means of transmission of those negative energies to you. It is important that you cut all cords of connections regularly, and free yourself.

WAYS TO CUT CORDS OF CONNECTION

1. If you have a specific person in mind that you have a strong connection with, or you feel that someone is jealous or sends negative energy your way, this is the method to do it. Bring that person in your mind. The source of connection usually is on your belly button. Imagine your hand is a knife and "cut" the invisible connection cord three times with a firm movement, in front of your belly button. Say "Cut, cut, cut". Then imagine the dark energy from that cord burning away.

2. Archangel Michael can cut any such cords anytime you feel drained.

> *"I call upon Archangel Michael; please help me by cutting any cords of attachments that affect my state of being, and life. Please cut them now so they don't have an effect on my any more. Thank you, and so it is."*

3. Work with your higher self. Through the Akashic records, you can delete any cords. Simply ask your higher self.

> *"I now declare that no cords of attachments with anyone can affect me today. I release and let go of any people, events and circumstances that have a negative effect to me. I cut them now. thank you and so it is."*

Imagine that you are showered with wave of release. You should feel lighter.

39. HOW TO MAXIMIZE YOUR PHYSICAL STRENGHT

The strength of our physical body is in fact directed by our minds. Since our mind is filled with our ego, thoughts and beliefs we limit our physical strength consciously or unconsciously.

Our physical strength helps us to lift weights, run fast and so on. If you find the power within, you can activate at will and maximize your physical abilities and strength. Great masters have acknowledged this and there are martial arts based on this technique. No, it doesn't need muscle; you only need to direct the energy of your body.

Try the following steps and you will find it exceptional and easy.

STEPS TO MAXIMIZE YOUR PHYSICAL STRENGHT

1. Find a heavy object such as furniture and try to lift it. Of course don't choose an object that weights tons; we will only try to maximize your physical strength not give you superpowers! We are not messing with laws of physics; only discover your exceptional energy strength.

As you try to lift this item, observe how heavy it is and how up, you can lift it.

2. Tune into your inner and outer energy. See with your mind's eye the energy of your physical body moving through you. For this exercise you are not going to use your muscles but your energy. As you see your energy in your mind's eye, you summon it in your hands. Visualize the energy move from the center of your spine to your hands.

3. Release any expectations, thoughts or fear and the energy now in your hands; get ready to lift the object. Close your eyes see the energy one more time, moving to your arms and hands, feel the energy of your body making you stronger like this, lift the object as up as you can.

4. Open your eyes and notice how far up you lifted this item.

Usually, this technic gets better with practice. The key is to let go of thoughts, and not use your muscles, but the energy of your body. The same technique can be used for any physical ability, like running fast, jumping high, swimming faster and so forth.

40. HOW TO CONNECT WITH SPIRIT THROUGH AUTOMATIC WRITING

If you want to connect with spirit and receive Divine guidance and communication, automatic writing is the best technique to try in the beginning. It does not require necessary skills, only the process of quieting your mind. In a few words, automatic writing is transcribing your thoughts that are guided by spirit.

Automatic writing, or unconscious writing, is the process of writing down thoughts that are inspired by spirit. It is not dangerous and it is fun. The more you use it, the more you skill your spirit communication and you will soon be able to use "channeling spirit" as in chapter 49.

If you haven't tried any spirit communication before, I would suggest starting out with automatic writing with your own higher voice. As your higher self is already a part of you, connection can be established more easily. As you craft that connection, you can then easily talk with your Angels, guides and any loving spirit you desire. If you are wondering about this Higher Self, they are a Divine part of you that is still in spirit, and has the wisdom from all your other lifetimes. They are in connection with your spiritual team of guides and Angels that guide and help all the time. They are very wise, so don't hesitate to ask them any questions.

Before you begin, I would suggest you meditate a few minutes as this will help you to quiet your mind and allow a clearer communication. For even better connection, spent some time raising your vibration (chapter 5), to ensure it is high enough to match Divine frequency.

For this technique you will need a piece of paper and pen. When you have some peace and quiet, let's begin.

STEPS TO CONNECTING WITH SPIRIT THROUGH AUTOMATIC WRITING

1. For a better connection, I suggest lighting up a candle, put some meditation music on, burn an essential oil, and/or have crystals close to you.

2. It is always a good idea to call Archangel Michael for some protection.

"Archangel Michael of the light, I call upon you now to shield me with your protective light and remove any negative energy or spirits from connecting with me. Thank you, and so it is."

3. We begin with an invocation to allow spirit to connect with us. First decide which spirit you want to begin with, and then say this simple invocation:

"I ask to connect with the most loving spirit, that can most assist me at this time/with my loving higher self/ (or name your spirit) please connect with me as clearly as possible, and help me write your words on paper. It is my intention that I distinguish them as clearly as possible. Thank you, and so it is."

4. Allow a few seconds to merge their energy with yours. Close your eyes and breath in and out clearing your mind. Then, start by writing your first question on paper. Now be ready to write down any thought that comes to mind. Spirit sends you words similar to your own thinking, so do not worry if you are uncertain, write them all down and do not judge or wonder. Also do not try to come up with the answer, simply relax your mind and do not allow yourself to think. Thoughts from spirit come naturally as soon as we clear our own.

5. As you write the answer to your first question, keep writing down any questions and the responses that come immediately through your thoughts. Do not pause to consider or doubt them, let go of your expectations and doubts and distinguish your own ego from the answers, at least until you finish transcribing their response.

6. When you finish, thank your spirit and congratulate yourself for a great connection.

WAYS TO DISTINGUISH SPIRIT COMMUNICATION

As I already mentioned, spirit communication through automatic writing is simple since you receive the answers through your own thoughts. For this, you can easily doubt your own responses from those of spirit. I know I was confused all the time at first and in doubt whether those responses were indeed coming from spirit. Therefore, I let you on some tips as to how to distinguish them.

a. The biggest clue is the content. How can you know the answer to such questions? You were the one that asked the questions right? So who could you know? What I like to do is to consider each question, pause and a few seconds and try to come up with the answer on my own. Then after I receive the answer from spirit I am certain I was unaware of this answer before.

b. Feeling. The responses from Divine beings are usually associated with loving emotions. Also the content of the thought is always loving, soothing, inspiring, even if it is not the answer we were hoping for. On the contrary, our ego self might come up with the answers that bring judgment, fear, uncertainty.

c. With A LOT of practice, you will distinguish differences from your own thoughts than with the thoughts that are spirit inspired. I discovered that my thoughts feel they come from the front section of the brain, whilst from spirit; thoughts come from the center of the brain. I know this can easily confuse you, but practice makes perfect.

d. Repetition. At some point, your ego brings automatic responses back to you. It tries to fill the gap of quiet and answer any questions so you are not left with any responses. What I found interesting is that after a while, we began familiar with the way spirit communicates, and the ego imitates that loving voice. This is when it gets trickier to distinguish the two. However, the ego does not know the answers; it only uses our memory to respond. This gets a lot of the same responses for different questions.

• Since we want to receive guidance from spirit, we sometimes worry whether spirit will communicate, of if they get frustrated and so forth. For this we rush to think the answers first. Every time you ask a question, relax and trust that spirit will answer, and it loves to connect with us. It might take longer some times, but this is because spirit tries to come through. If we are worried or we have low energy, they try to raise our energy so they can come through. Like a radio signal, the more peaceful and happy we are, the clearer we get the frequency.

• If you try to communicate with a deceased loved one in this way, do not get discouraged if they do not communicate. Spirits that are passed may not be as strong to connect with us in this way. If you try to connect with a deceased spirit, I suggest connecting with your spirit guides or Angels instead and asking them to pass on messages or ask them directly, they may know the answers.

• Spirits help you understand, help to guide and instruct you but they NEVER intervene with your free will. They can't tell you what to do decide if you are in doubt, but help you find the answer within. They also don't know what will happen in the future, as that yet unknown.

• Better questions, better answers. Form your questions as clearly as possible and be as specific as you can so you get a satisfying answer. If ask general questions, you get general answers.

PART 3:

SPIRITUAL MASTERS

41. HOW TO MOVE FROM THE 3RD TO THE 5TH DIMENSION

This world is changing. It gradually shifts energy from fear that was dominant through so many years on earth, into love. Fifth dimension is a spiritual ascension that holds pure energies, closer to source or God. This energy shifts as more of us become awakened by our spirit, and Divine nature. Our energy level expands, and along with it, it restores earth's purified energy.

The move from the third to the fifth dimension benefits all of us and it will ultimately shift all humanity. If you haven't read my previous book "The truth of all that is" you are probably wondering what does this new dimension entails. For humans, it means letting go of their ego side, so the soul can thrive. The effects of this change are plenty, some evident and some not. We are happier, more align with our divinity, closer to the Angels and God, more carefree, prosperous, and more in control of our fate. We emanate love and care for others, and for earth.

Those that have already expanded in the fifth dimension, they will find the practices of this book easier than others, and be more successful in their practices. This is because they are closer to their Divine nature. If you are ready to expand your soul, and diminish the ego self, read along the methods of this chapter.

WAYS TO EXPAND TO THE 5ᵀᴴ DIMENSION

1. **Meditate**. As you meditate, you let go of your ego side and emerge with your spirit that is your divinity. You allow the connection to become bigger each time.

2. **Detox**. This is not food or addictions detox, but detox from negative people that drain you. When you try to raise your vibration and there are people who whine, cry, judge they pull you right down again. On this path, you have to let go of some "friends" as your energies no longer match and they only bring you down. Don't let them keep you grounded, lovingly avoid interaction with them.

3. **Be yourself**. Do not restrain who you are; all you are beautiful. You have to love yourself just like you are because this is the way your higher self sees you, perfect. Stand in front of the mirror and compliment yourself inside and out.

4. **Forgiveness**. If you have hate or judgment in your heart you are not going to thrive. You must let it go as this ego side that needs holds you back. You will find chapter 25 useful.

5. **Raise your vibration**. The happier you are, the more you become a math to spirit. Fly high, be happy and don't let anyone bring you down. (See chapter 5).

6. **Be around people with raised energy.** Energy transmits from one person to the other. Be around people that make you happy and help you be who you are with no judgment.

7. **Music**. Music helps to soothe and clear your mind. It also uplifts your energy. Find high vibrational music and listen to it regularly to relax, and uplift towards love and happiness.

8. **Do what you love**. This goes without saying but if you stress and worry all the time, you don't allow yourself to thrive. Also let go of anything that drains you physically and emotionally. This may a job, people, or a task.

9. **Don't watch T.v.** Avoid anything that brings you down, and that is watching the news, or any T.v for that matter. If you want to watch something, choose something pleasant. I used to love watching thriller movies for instance, I don't anymore. They drain my energy and create unpleasant emotion. I only watch comedies.

10. **Be around nature and animals.** The more time you spent with them, the more you uplift and recharge.

11. **Don't gossip or judge**. This is ego self-doing. It holds you back from your ascension.

12. **Practice connecting with spirit**. Whether you try a divination tool, or channeling, the interaction with lighted beings helps you uplift in higher realms.

13. **Work with the Angels.** Pray, channel, invoke them as they help us reach our Divine side.

Try a combination of the techniques and you will feel lighter and better.

Symptoms that you have entered into the fifth dimension:

a. **Headaches**. Higher vibrations mean that you need some time to adjust.

b. **Ear buzzing.** You will find your ears being blocked or buzzing or you will be more sensitive to sounds.

c. **Interrupted sleep patterns**. As you try to get used to the change, you might wake up regularly from deep sleep.

d. **Mood swings.** You might be feeling down and suddenly very happy or the opposite.

e. **Change**. Change of path, job, environment or friends. Of course this is a shift towards the better.

g. **Lack of concentration.** This happens a lot as well, you can't stay in one task for long.

h. **Losing sense of time**. In 5d or the spirit world, time does not exist. You will find yourself checking the clock regularly not to miss any appointments as time seems to drifting away.

i. **Heightened sensitivity** towards taste, smell, sounds.

g. Happiness and love. These feelings come regularly and they are strong within you.

42. HOW TO OPEN YOUR THIRD EYE

Third eye refers to an invisible eye that offers insight beyond ordinary sight. If you train and clear your third eye, you are able to receive guidance from spirit, be in connection with your higher self, expand your consciousness, receive inspiration, creativity and even be able to see, or hear spirit. It is in other words, your 6th sense ability.

As you open your third eye, you awake your sixth sense. With that, you can easily acquire any clair ability, or even all of them. Some may be more skilled with one ability, but you can in fact acquire and skill them all.

The clair abilities are means of connection with spirit.

CLAIRVOYANCE is the ability to see mental images which are perceived without the use of physical eyes.

CLAIRAUDIENCE ability entails perceiving sounds or words without a noise that occurs mentally from spirit.

CLAIRSENTIENCE means clear sensation or feeling that again, is guided by spirit.

CLAIRSCENT is clear smelling odors that have no physical source.

CLAIRTANGENCY is clear touching or psychometry. People with this ability receive information simply by touch.

CLAIRGUSTANCE means clear tasting, without tasting any physical food.

CLAIREMPATHY is clear emotion. An Empath can feel the emotion of a person, place or animal.

Third eye is located in the middle of your forehead. It holds the ability to receive and translate spiritual connection. When we are born, third eye is open, cleared, and able to perceive spirits, and light orbs. How many times did come upon a child that speaks or plays with their "imaginary" friends. The truth is, they are not imaginary. Children are able to sense or even see spirits that they can easily befriend. Like I mentioned in earlier chapters, there is no need to fear spirits, as they cannot harm the living. Ultimately, in time, fear takes over children close their third eye communication. This chapter is to help you open it up again.

Opening up your third eye, does not entail being able to see ghosts running around, but being able to perceive any Divine signs and messages, inspiration and presence. The clearer the connection with spirit, the more inspiration and assistance we receive. The great thing about your spirit guides and Angels is that they exist in the non-physical to protect from any unwanted interactions. So if you ask them to be wary and not allow any spirit to communicate with you, then they stand like guards protecting you. This way, it is unlikely you will see any spirits such as ghosts floating around, unless of course you want to.

Let go of your fear. Understand that there is nothing to worry about; there is nothing evil or malicious wanting to harm you. When you understand and let go of this fear, then you will feel more comfortable and ready to experience the third eye opening. If however you worry constantly, then the third eye will remain closed. Opening and clearing your third eye, entails letting go of any fears that have blocked it. If your third eye was going to reveal scary, dangerous spirits or worlds, why were we born with our third eye open? It is natural, safe, and healthy for it to be open and cleared.

The very first step for third eye opening is intention. Ask beforehand in your mind or out loud, that you want to clear, open or unblock your third eye. Subsequent, try some of the methods below.

WAYS TO OPEN UP YOUR THIRD EYE

1. **Mantra**: The mantra "Thoh" can unlock any energy blocking the third eye area.

a. Breathe in and hold your breath for a while. Place the tip of your tongue between your slightly parted teeth. Release your breath slowly through your mouth, pronouncing the word "Thoh" as you exhale.

b. Repeat five times, repeating the mantra with each exhale.

c. repeat this exercise for three days, at the same time.

2. **Archangel Michael**. Calling for Archangel Michael will help you in releasing any fears, and energy on that area.

"Archangel Michael, please join me now and clear away all negative energy, fears or beliefs regarding my third eye. Please cleanse and energize my third eye, so I can experience its advantages with peace and love. Thank you for all your kind assistance, thank you, thank you. So be it."

Rest or meditate, and allow Archangel Michael to work on your third eye clearing.

3. **Visualization**. Close your eyes and relax. Visualize a white clearing light emerging from the sky, and filling your third eye area. Know that this white light helps to diminish any negative energy, fears or false perceptions so that it becomes unblocked. See this white light emanating brightness, feel its energy on your forehead as a gentle tickling. Allow it to work on you, as you focus on taking long deep breaths.

Now the white light absorbs all negative energy and returns back to the sky.

4. **Spiritual team work:** ask your higher self and your guides. Tell them out loud:

> *"Higher self and spiritual team of spirit guides, Angels, ascended masters, loving spirits. I am ready to unblock my third eye and experience my sixth sense. Please work with me while I sleep, delete and clear any negative programs that may block my third eye and help me open up to its glory. Thank you, and so it is."*

5. **Crystal healing**. Adding a crystal on your third eye, it will absorb any blockages. For how to use, clear or direct crystals, go to chapter ___.

> **a**. Cleanse your crystals. Preferably for this, choose: clear quartz, Indigo Kyanite, or amethyst.
>
> **b**. Hold your crystal in your right hand and direct it on the job done. "It is my intention that you successfully unblock and open my third eye."
>
> **c**. Place the crystal in the middle of your forehead. Lie down, meditate or relax for at least thirty minutes.
>
> **d**. When you are done cleanse your stone.

It is a good idea to try a combination of the methods above. Repeat each process for 5 days and if you don't experience anything different, repeat with another technique.

THIRD EYE OPENING SYMPTOMS

When you third eye opens you will feel a change. The most common ones are the symptoms below:

a. **Head pressure**. You might experience pressure in the head, especially in the center of your forehead. This is a sign that your pineal gland that is in the center of your head, is growing energetically.

b. **Headaches**. You are sensitive to energies since now your brain begins to function differently. Don't worry it is normal simply relax and allow it time to pass.

c. **Sound sensitivity**. High pitched sounds will annoy you, you might find yourself enjoying soothing, low tunes.

d. **Light sensitivity.** No you won't turn into a vampire! Since your third eye opens, you will be exposed to a new set of images like orbs; aura colors and so forth, for this any light might feel intense until you new "eye perspective" gets adjusted.

e. Increased intuition. You will get a knowing about what is beneficial or even insight on people you just met. This will happen as a knowing, that will guide you from within.

f. Crowd sensitivity. This is the one that I received as the more intense sign of my third opening. You won't be able to handle a big crowd for a long period of time. This is because you are sensitive to energies and more people mean different energies and vibrations. You will soon want to take a run from all the noises and people who are governed by their ego, or they are full of pessimism.

A word of caution, you will soon change friends that don't share the same views as you. As you grow energetically, it is only natural to not be a match with certain people that only bring you down. Go for it, it is in fact a blessed change.

43. HOW TO CLOSE YOUR THIRD EYE

Not all people can handle the changes that they will face once their third eye is open. Someone who is not yet ready emotionally will not benefit from the extrasensory perceptions that they will acquire. I have heard a lot of instances of people that were frightened from seeing orbs, or hearing intuitive sounds. This goes without saying that you should be prepared to expand spiritually, and not be afraid to actually receive signs from your spirit guides.

Not all people have difficulty adjusting of course. I for instance didn't have any scary or annoying effects. It happened gradually and it gave me time to adjust and learn. Symptoms occurred one at a time and I always had Angel protection so I wasn't afraid. You will slowly find your own rhythm and the experiences you gain might be different from others.

It is understandable however, to fear the unknown. You gain all these knew experiences and you become extra sensitive to energies and to spirits. If all these new vibrations make you seek then it is wise to take a step back and close your third eye again until you are ready to work through the changes.

WAYS TO CLOSE YOUR THIRD EYE

1. Visualize your third eye as a big and bright lotus flower. In a relaxed state, focus on your breathing, and then imagine that third eye flower slowly closing and capturing its light within. Repeat the visualization for seven days.

2. Intention and team protection. Ask your guides to step in and help you. They don't want you to be afraid or worried so they can help you adjust to the new energies or, direct your third eye to close.

44. HOW TO DEVELOP YOUR CLAIRAUDIENT ABILITY

Clairaudience is the ability to receive mental words through spirit, similar to your own thoughts. People with this ability can also train their ears to perceive spirit sounds that occur in higher frequencies.

You can clearly communicate with spirit through clairaudience ability. Spirit forms energy that you translate as words through your own thoughts. To enhance this skill, you must be open, receptive and connected with your higher self. The more connected you are, the more you can understand high frequency energies and translate them. Another valuable step is to comprehend and differentiate words that come from spirit, and your own thoughts. Clairaudience ability may seem as something difficult at first, but everyone can attain this ability as you train yourself to receive the frequency of spirit.

To be able to perceive, and understand sounds coming from higher realms, you should get acquainted with higher frequencies that spirit communication occurs. To do this, you must practice meditation, and channeling on a frequent basis.

Clairaudent ability usually occurs within your mind, through your thoughts. However as you craft it, you may be able to perceive external sounds as well. As you train your ears, you tune into higher frequencies that other physical ears might not be able to listen. As I crafted my clairaudient ability, I was able to capture songs with my physical ears. In fact, I listened to a choir of Angels, was humming a tune. I heard this beautiful song, every day when I was at my office. This went on for days and it truly was magical. Of course at first I didn't know what it was, or where it came from. The more I listened to the song, the more relaxed I became and the more my vibrations rose.

Having this ability enhanced can be truly fulfilling.

WAYS TO TRAIN YOUR CLAIRAUDIENT ABILITY

1. Meditation. I was able to receive mental communication through meditation. I meditated for half hour, every day. After two months or so, I achieved a calm state of mind, and I could differentiate my thoughts, from the words of spirit.

 I suggest you find a time through the day, and practice meditation daily. I suggest half hour at least five days a week. Find a great calming tune and meditate as you hear the music. I don't suggest guided meditations for this training, as you would need to learn to calm your thoughts on your own. Refer to chapter 1 for tips on meditation.

2. Listen. Train your ears to pay attention to sounds. As you listen, you silence all thoughts. Listen to all external sounds. This is the key to a clear mental communication.

Take note of all sounds: wind, birds, people, trees and so on.

3. Ask and listen. Think of a radio. You try to pick up the right frequency to listen to a song. Similarly, with this method, you try to tune into higher consciousness. The only way to do this is, is if you listen.

     a. Call upon your guardian Angel, or your higher voice to communicate with you clearly.

     "My loving guardian Angel, please connect with me through mental hearing and help me understand your responses."

     b. Ask a question you are interested in.

     c. Listen. Try to find the frequency of your guardian Angel. Allow your own thoughts to disappear and be replaced with the ones that your Angels send out.

     d. Something to I like to do is speak the words I get out loud. This helps me understand them clearly, and differentiate them from my own tone of voice.

     e. Try again and again. The more you allow yourself to connect, the higher frequencies you can translate. Don't give up. You are slowly climbing the ladder to higher levels of communication.

4. Imagine sounds. This exercise helps you to translate sounds. Try to mentally hear sounds from memory.

How does a piano sound? A violin? What about the ocean? Hear a wooden floor that creaks, a church bell, a phone ringing. You get the idea. Mentally hear any sounds you can think of to train your mental hearing.

When you are ready for spirit communication with your clairaudient ability, try the steps in chapter 44.

45. HOW TO DEVELOP CLAIRVOYANCE

Clairvoyance is the ability to receive mental images from spirit. These images may bring you guidance, answers to your questions or support. Working with clairvoyance is a two way technique: perceiving the images and understanding their meaning through intuition.

"Third eye" is located in between the eyebrows and it is responsible for the mental images that we receive. We all have this, but for many it is blocked and some have difficulty receiving mental images at first. To open your third eye, reference chapter _____.

Working on your clairvoyance skill can be very fulfilling. No don't worry you will not see ghosts flying around. You can easily control your sight and only allow certain spirits to connect with you at will. I for instance, only allow my third eye to open when I channel, or heal. I have never seen any ghosts, but I have seen orbs and energy.

Clairvoyant images are mostly mental images, similar to the ones you create when you use your imagination. Nevertheless, you don't initiate those images but they suddenly arise in your mind. You might get a glimpse of them, and often they may not be as vivid. As you practice your clairvoyant ability those images will last longer and become clearer.

Usually you will get images in combination with a knowing of what they mean. Other times, an image will be associated with a thought just to help you understand better, or the opposite.

A recent clairvoyant example is when spirits were trying to tell me that someone was "stuck" in their path the image they showed was a circle telling me in other words that this person seems to be going in circles and not moving forward. Similarly, they sometimes choose to convey images in combination with other clair abilities.

Also, Clairvoyance can be very helpful to someone who is a healer. As they tune in to their clairvoyant ability, they can see auras and immediately spot a physical problem from the aura abnormality.

WAYS TO DEVELOP CLAIRVOYANT ABILITY

1. **Work with the Angels**. First thing you have to do is clear any blockages that might prevent you from fully experiencing mental images. Ask for Archangel Michael and Archangel Haniel to step in and assist you.

> *"I call for the loving Archangel Michael and Archangel Haniel, please join me and assist me to clear away any negative energy and blockages from my third eye in order to experience and benefit from my clairvoyance. Thank you, and so it is."*

2. *Affirmation. Repeat the phrase: "I am highly clairvoyant" as often as you can. (See chapter 22 on how to use affirmations) in this way you imprint it into your subconscious that responds with clairvoyant abilities.*

3. **Visualization.** Keep practicing visualization (see chapter 23) because as you create mental images in your mind you also practice perceiving them. the following images in as much detail as you can:

- A bucket of beautiful colorful flowers.

- A calm ocean scene while the sun sets.

- Children playing on the playground.

- The sky with white puffy clouds and birds flying.

4. Intention. Release fears that may block your clairvoyant insight. Pray to your guides and Angels to help you see through your third eye.

> *"I ask for my higher self, spiritual team and all Angels that can most help at this time. I am ready to experience my clairvoyant abilities. Help me release any fears that are blocking my insight, help me see through my third eye and understand your messages. Thank you and so it is."*

As you do this, relax and close your eyes. Ask your guides to show you any images or messages and trust what you receive. Keep practicing and your vision will get better in time.

5. Meditation. Relax and set your intention before you begin. "I want to receive clear mental images as an answer to this question: _____". Now meditate and be aware of any images.

A good exercise is to work with your guides for practice. Ask them to help you see something that will happen later that day. You might see just a color, or an item. As you go by your day, lay alert for any images that resemble what you saw.

46. HOW TO SEE ANGELS

As you already know, Angels do not have a physical form; they exist in the thirteenth plane and they are energy. If we see them with our physical eyes, all we would capture are orbs of light.

The Angels choose to appear to us at will. We may sense them as unconditional love, a breeze, we might see them in a dream or they can take forms on very rare occasions as apparitions. When they do, they know we associate them with wings, so they make take a similar form.

Angels can be present at many places at once, and they always know when they are being called. They never interfere with our free will, but they can bring assistance through signs, inspiration or through others.

You may also have heard instances of words spoken that saved someone. For instance, "watch out", or "take the other road", or similar words that get our attention, and are enough to save us from death. Those are very rare occasions that they intervene when it is a matter of life of death.

In this chapter, I want to help you see Angels through physical eyes. What you will be able to capture however, is mostly energy, or orbs of light. Trust that the Angels are with you and if you see them, congratulate yourself for tuning into their energy.

Similar to hearing a spirit sound, you have to adjust your eyes to see on higher planes, and this will require practice. For this task, we ask Angels to level a bit closer to our own dimension, in order to be able to perceive them more easily.

STEPS TO SEE AN ANGEL

1. Meditate first, to calm your mind, or try this technique right after you wake up when your mind is relaxed and cleared.

2. Ask for protection or invoke protective light. See chapter 4.

3. Invoke an Angel to stand in front of you. Choose a white background, as this will help you adjust on their aura more easily.

> *"I ask the most loving Angel that can assist at this time, please help me see you through my physical eyes. Stand in front of me and help me see your form. Thank you, and so it is."*

4. Concentrate on the space in front of you. Listen to your emotions. Usually when you are near an Angel, your vibration gets greater.

Try to make out an invisible aura at first. Then, you will be able to see more details like colors.

5. Don't try this for long as you will strain your eyes. Don't get frustrated with yourself if you can't see anything. Know that there is indeed an Angel in front of you, and you will be able to see them when your eyes adjust.

For better results try third eye activation first on chapter 42.

If you were not able to see an Angel, try chapter 46 feeling an Angel. Your eyes may take more to adjust, but even so, if you don't believe, you won't be able to see their energy. Feeling them is easier, and it will enhance your believe so you can achieve this more easily.

47. HOW TO USE A CRYSTAL BALL

Crystal ball scrying or gazing, is another method that people use to interpret messages from spirit. It has been used through hundreds of years and it can be a helpful tool to your spiritual communication.

The way you use a crystal ball is simple. You stare at the clear ball and interpret the shadows or images you capture through it. You see images through the ball while in a trance state, but they come through your third eye, similar to the clairvoyant ability. In brief, it is like you enter into meditation, with your eyes open, staring at the ball. What you see comes from the celestial plane as answers to your questions mentally, like a vision and not as physical images through the crystal ball.

Much like pendulum dowsing and card reading, you use the ball as a tool, but you are the one interpreting the messages. You rely on your intuition and not on symbols or words. Much similarly to tea leaves reading, or coffee reading, that your grandma uses to read, you try to interpret the images that you see. It requires skill and insight.

Not all clear balls work as a divination tool. Glass is obviously cheaper, but clear quartz can interpret energy more easily.

Similarly to any crystal, you can direct it to give you accurate images, clear it and energize it. See chapter 3 for handling crystals.

The method below is very simple but you can find other methods, or more detailed ways to interpret the messages.

STEPS TO CRYSTAL BALL GAZING

1. Cleanse your crystal and direct it to help you find answers to what you are searching for through crystal gazing.

2. Light a white or purple candle behind you, but still allow some light to shine in the ball.

3. Go through a protection process. See chapter 4.

4. Invoke lighted beings such as Angels to help you see images through the ball.

> *"I lovingly invoke loving Angels to help me see and interpret messages through this crystal ball. Speak to me through it, direct me, raise my vibration so that I can understand the messages that you bring. Thank you, and so it is."*

5. Hold the ball with two hands to charge it with your energy. Ask your question.

6. Relax, let go of the ball and just stare at it while a meditative state. Clear away any thoughts as they intervene with your reading. To accurately use a crystal ball, you should be in a deep trance state as you allow the messages to form through your mind, and see their reflection on the ball.

7. You might see smoke forming; allow pictures to form within the ball one after the other.   Choose the clearest image first. At this point don't try to interpret their meaning, but understand what images are formed.

8. Keep choosing images and focus on them, trying to answer your imposed question. It helps to have a diary to take a note of the images as they form, or a recorder to speak out loud what you see.

9. When there are no more images, you can pause and try to interpret what you saw. Your Angels always help you through this part through intuition. You will receive a deeper knowing as to what the messages are.

Remember, with practice you become better.

48. HOW TO READ ENERGY THROUGH A PICTURE

Reading energy through a picture means connecting spiritually with that person, getting a sense of what they feel, how they are like, and what spirits are attached with them. The information that comes through is mostly random, not directed at will, and it has to do with the energies that affect the person at that time. For instance they may feel tired, or they go through a hard time, or they have thoughts of buying a new car. With this kind of an energy reading, you get what is going on with them through the energies that are dominant in or around them. This is why I call it energy reading.

Many people have spirits attached to them. This may be a lost loved one, or a spirit that has an attachment with them. When you connect with that person, you also connect with their spirit (I know I do). The spirits that are with them know that you try to connect with that person and they may direct you by giving you information for each reading.

Energy reading is a great practice to expand your intuition.

You need permission before you tune into anyone's energy, because you are tuning into their life. If you did not ask permission, their guides will block much information so you may not be able to receive any energy for the reading.

STEPS TO READ ENERGY THROUGH A PICTURE

1. Ask a person willing to get an energy reading with you, permission. It works better with someone you don't know, as you will refer on your intuition and not on what you already know about them. This way, you can then test and see how many things you got right.

2. Ask the person to give you a recent picture that shows their eyes clearly, preferably a picture with only their face and shoulders. It is important that they are alone in the picture you try to read, unless other people's energies may interfere with your reading.

3. Protection. As you have already noticed, I always invoke protection before I silence my thoughts. See chapter 4 for ways to do that.

4. Ask your guides to help you with the reading.

> *"I ask my higher self and spiritual team to help me read the energy of _____ accurately. I ask for __the persons'_____ guides to reveal any information will help her/him at this time. Thank you, and so it is."*

5. Focus on the picture. The parts that hold the most energy are usually the eyes and the forehead. However, follow your gaze and fixate in whatever area you feel drawn to. This process is to establish a connection between you and the person, so you can receive information through your higher self.

6. Your higher self begins to send you information mainly through your intuition. You need to silence all thoughts in order to understand the guidance. At this point a thought comes in your mind. It may be completely random, there may not be a way for you to know this, yet your intuition lets you know.

You might get thoughts like, "You have a brother, that brother has a big influence or you," or "is your father passed? He is with you now."

At one time I even got a message that this woman has an orange vase in her attic. I had no way of knowing this, but her son who passed away was with her at that time, and he gave me that information. Spirits can be cheeky like that. You may receive anything; let the information come and trust that it is true. The key is to trust your intuition. The more you rely on it, the stronger and clearer it becomes.

In time, you can focus the reading on certain areas or questions and you will be able to receive information either from the spirits that surround them, or through their guides and higher self.

7. Validate all the information you have received through the person you give reading to. This way you know how many of the things were correct. With practice, you will get most of them right.

8. At the end of a reading, I encourage you to cut the cords of connection with them, so you stop receiving information and you break the interaction with their guides. See chapter 38.

You may not be able to receive all information right. That is alright, as you try to translate energy, sometimes the messages are not as clear. Don't focus on what you didn't get right, but be happy with those you did get and congratulate yourself.

49. HOW TO CHANNEL SPIRIT

The following process is to allow Divine frequencies to communicate with you in order to pass on messages, guidance and wisdom from spirit. To be able to connect with spirit directly, first practice quieting your mind through meditation, as this will allow spirit communication through your thoughts. Quieting your mind will also help you to distinguish spirit communication from your own thoughts.

Channeling requires practice so do not get discouraged if you are not able to achieve Divine communication immediately. I suggest you try spirit communication through automatic writing first, as it is an easier technique for beginners. Find automatic writing on chapter 40.

I strongly advise you to only allow spirit communication with lighted beings like Angels, ascended masters, spirit guides or known lost loved one. If you allow spirits to connect with you, and do not take protection measures, any kind of spirit can connect that might draw your energy or become attached to you. For this, the steps I entail below have an extra protection measure, against any other spirits.

What to expect:

Channeling is not possession. Possession is a very negative term that entails you did not give permission to "lend" your body or thoughts, and you do not have the free will to regain them. It also entails you don't have any control. Channeling is very different and not dangerous at all, especially if you use protection. With channeling, you quiet your own thoughts so you can distinguish vibrations given by spirit. Lighted spirits do not possess a vessel but are happy to use our consciousness to pass on messages or to help us progress. When you channel a spirit, you feel high Ethereal energy, upliftment. You willingly ask them to connect, and they do not take a hold of your body or mind. You are present and aware at the moment of channeling, even though the thoughts or movements you receive are guided by spirit.

Channeling occurs through many of the clair abilities linked together in a strong high vibrational connection. Some people might receive only thoughts or only images and later on they enhance their communication with more clair abilities. Also some spirits may choose to connect with one way or the other; it does not always depend on your skills but sometimes is a spirit preference.

When you connect clairaudiently, thoughts come that are then translated into words but it happens almost simultaneous. You never know what they might say once you begin to speak their words. Similarly, with images and the clairvoyant ability you may ask a question and see an image that is associated with a knowing as they help you to understand those images. The images you capture however might be symbolic.

When connection is established in a channeling, you will be in a trance state, as spirit takes over your ability to communicate. Communication can happen within your mind only, or it can be spoken out loud, it depends what you prefer. A successful channeling also entails that some movements are also controlled by spirit; you act them out unconsciously as you try to convey a meaning. Your tone of voice might change, the way you speak might as well, you may even speak with an accent. It all depends on the spirit you are connecting and how clearly you channel them. Think of it like a radio station, the clearer the station, the better the music.

You will have full consciousness and ability to control your thoughts and movements of course, but the deeper the connection, the more difficult will be for you to discuss with spirit verbally. I love to ask spirit questions through my thoughts as they always know and respond. Most importantly you can end the communication in any time you want. Your free will is the key.

Before you begin, meditate for a few minutes first; as this will help you quiet your mind and allow a clearer communication.

STEPS TO CHANNELING SPIRIT

The key to connecting with lighted beings is your frequency. If you are low, sad, upset or angry, you attract spirits with similar vibration. Before you connect or channel with any spirit, take a few minutes to raise your vibration (see chapter 5) and de-clutter your space (see chapter 9).

1. Cleanse your space and yourself first (see chapter 4)

2. Light a candle, burn some essential oils, have some crystals around, or on you to help increase spirit connection. This step is not necessary but it definitely helps.

3. Create some questions for your spirit to answer beforehand because unless someone is with you to form questions, it will be difficult to discuss with spirit directly (but not impossible).

4. Get some recording equipment ready to document all the answers.

5. Before any invocation, I always call on Archangel Michael for protection.

> *"Archangel Michael of the light, I call upon you now to shield me with your protective light and remove any negative energy or spirits from connecting with me. Thank you, and so it is."*

Decide who you would like to connect with. Bear in mind that usually spirits come together and are presented as one energy. You don't have to connect with a specific spirit if you don't have anyone in mind, simply allow one to come forth that can most assist you.

You can connect with anyone you want, your higher self, your guardian Angel, any Archangel, Mother Mary, any ascended master, or even Mother Teresa. The energy of each spirit is different. The energy of an Archangel will be stronger than the energy of your guardian Angel. A stronger energy will connect with you more clearly, but it will also vibrate in a much higher level than you that you are not yet accustomed. Remember that different spirits have different energy and way of communication. Clairvoyance might see spirits in different colors, or clairaudience capture the connection in a different frequency.

When you are ready invoke them with this simple prayer:

"I call forth the most loving spirit that can most assist me at this time / (or name your spirit), to connect with me and answer my questions. I only ask lighted beings to surround me, and help me channel as clearly as possible, for the greatest and highest good of all. I allow you to do so, now. Thank you for connecting with me. And so it is."

8. Remove any thoughts and try to raise your vibration. Smile and allow them to work with your energy. It usually takes several seconds as they try to match your own energy with theirs. If your energy is not high enough, you will not be able to channel them clearly. I found that several strong spirits such as Archangels might take a little longer to connect as they share their own energy with yours to raise your frequency. The stronger the spirit, the better the communication, also, the higher energy you have and the better channeling you achieve. This step usually takes 60 seconds but it might take up to 10 minutes.

9. You will know connection is established when you sense a shift in vibration. Also you get high frequency emotions such as happiness, euphoria, unconditional love. Trust whatever you receive, the very first sentences may come up muffled, or you may not be sure a connection has been established. The very first words are the hardest to come through, once they do, the connection will become stronger. Speak the words you receive out loud, even if you are not sure they are them, it will become easier to tune into their energy in this way.

Usually at first they greet you, or begin answering your questions immediately. You can also ask them to help you understand that you are indeed receiving them. They may show you a sign or let you know with an image or word.

As I already mentioned earlier, there are two main ways of connection, mental thoughts or mental images. Embrace whatever way they appear.

10. Next is to let spirit answer your questions. Ask them and allow them time to respond. You can form the questions verbally or in your mind. Be open to whatever they may tell you and know they will NEVER discourage you or tell you what to do, or not do.

11. When you are ready to complete the channeling, all you have to do is let them know and thank them.

"Thank you for connecting with me and sharing your wisdom with me."

That, or something similar is enough to conclude the channeling.

- *If you try to communicate with a lost loved one in this way, do not get discouraged if they do not appear. Spirits that passed may not be as strong to connect with us in this way. If you try to connect with a lost spirit, I suggest connecting with your spirit guides or Angels instead and asking them to pass on messages or ask them directly, they may know the answers.*

- *Spirits help you understand guide and instruct you, but they NEVER intervene with your free will. They can't tell you what to do, but they help you find the answer within. They also don't know what will happen in the future, as that is yet unknown. What they get are only future possibilities.*

- *Better questions, better answers. Form your questions as clearly as possible and be as specific as you can so you get a satisfying answer. If ask general questions, you get general answers.*

50. HOW TO ASTRAL PROJECT

Astral projection, lucid dreaming or astral travel, are phrases to describe the same thing: Out of body experience. When this occurs, your soul separates from your body temporarily in order to travel in other places, time or dimensions. When we dream, our soul travels, but we are not conscious so we do not remember what we have experienced.

Astral projection requires skill and protection as souls can easily become disoriented from the various timelines and dimensions. On the other hand, there are endless experiences of people astral projecting every day consciously or unconsciously that can easily find their way. A link exists between soul and body that helps them to always stay connected and so the soul finds its way back at any time.

WAYS TO ASTRAL PROJECT:

1. **Protection:** Before going through any technique shield yourself. Use any of the methods in chapter 4.

2. Set a tim er. You need something to bring you back to the physical plane.

3. Intention and assistance. Set your intention to experience a successful astral projection. Decide where you want to go, and what you wish to see. Also, ask your guides and Angels to be present with you, to help you travel with ease.

> *"I ask my loving Angels and spirit guides, be present with me now, and help me to experience astral travel successfully. Help me to stay conscious, be with me to keep me safe and help me back to reality when I am ready. Thank you, thank you, thank you. And so it is."*

4. Lie down on your back; be as comfortable as you can.

Try any of the methods listed below until you find the one that was most successful to you.

For this method you need to be in a trance state. Release any fears before you begin. If you worry or hold negative emotions, the techniques will not be effective. Know that it is a safe place for you, and your guides and Angels are present to help you.

5. Choose one of the techniques below:

   a. The Rope Technique: Taken out of the teachings of Robert Bruce this is considered a very effective method.

   i. imagine an invisible rope hanging from your ceiling. Next, imagine that you climb this rope slowly. The more you climb, the more relaxed you get, and the more peaceful.

The higher you go, the more you will feel your body become numb or paralyzed. This is important in order to allow your soul to gently fly out of your physical body. Keep climbing the rope and allow yourself to relax some more. Once you are in a deep trance state, you will feel lighter.

ii. Create the intention of your soul moving outside or your body.

iii. You will feel being free from your body as you move away from the physical dimension.

iv. Think of where you want to go and what you want to see.

b. With your eyes closed, imagine your spiritual or astral body rising up from your physical, body. Keep repeating it clearly in your mind, until you feel like rising over your body. You may even see your physical body resting below you.

c. Wake up from your deep sleep at night, and hold the intention to astral travel. I suggest you set your alarm clock at 4:00 am. That time you are already relaxed from deep sleep, and you can easily let go of the physical body.

d. Tell yourself that you are going to sleep, but as you drift to sleep, maintain your awareness. When you feel that you are half sleeping try to move "out" of your body with movement.

e. Before you go to sleep create the intention that tonight you are lucid dreaming. Keep reminding yourself of this intention through the day to imprint it on the subconscious so that it guides you are in deep sleep.

If you are successful, you will find yourself lucid dreaming. This means that you will be aware you are sleeping but traveling. From there, you can direct your attention to move whenever you want to go. When you are done, tell yourself to return to the physical body and wake up.

If you succeed in waking up, write down all your experiences because chances are you are not going to remember them for long, or the details will fade.

f. Meditate until you are in a trance state. Then affirm:

"I am astral projecting, I let go of my awareness, I fly" to make your subconscious believe you are experiencing astral projection.

6. Ground yourself. This is a very important step to help you return to your physical body successfully. If you don't do this, you may feel out of place, dizzy or lightheaded. See grounding techniques in chapter 7.

- Astral projection needs crafting. In time you will succeed.

- Always, always, always ask for protection, also ask your guides to accompany you. As your soul flies it is quite fragile.

- A sign that you are astral projecting, or that you are ready to leave your body is a tingling sensation on your crown chakra. When this happens it means you are ready to leave your body. You have to roll out of your body, or simply stand up in a fast movement.

- Souls teleport from one place to the other. You won't have to go through a highway, or cross the sea like a bird. Be aware of where you want to go and voila; you are there.

- This is not a time for a channeling with your guides. You might see them with you, acknowledge them, but don't sit for a chat. You can do this when you meditate while you in your physical body as it is safer.

- When you astral project you can go anywhere! You can see your loved ones sleeping, or you can go back in time. For the future, you can visit one of your possible future pathways IF your guides allow it. You can also visit other planes, other lifetimes and so forth.

Please do share your experiences with me; I want to know what you have experienced! amelia@ameliabert.com

51. HOW TO CREATE SPIRITUAL ARTWORK

Before an artist begins to fill the canvas, they picture the project in their mind. They first have an image, and then they try to convey it on the project. Spiritual artwork is different, you are the artist, however you do not have the project in mind, but you allow spirit to guide you with every movement. To create a spiritual artwork, you must allow your thoughts to disappear in order to receive the inspiration from the Ether.

The great thing about working with spirit, is that you don't have to be an artist, nor need to have any artistic experience. You become a "vessel" that brings an art to the physical world. You allow spirit to become one with you at that moment, and you pass on the information it brings, without thought, without struggle, without knowing what it will be delivered. In an art project, you lent spirit your hands, and you follow the guidance that comes through the mind.

This topic is listed under "spiritual mastery" because you must first learn to communicate with spirit, and allow Divine assistance to guide you. When you do that, spiritual artwork becomes easy.

First, decide what form of art you will use. This can be done with anything, a pencil, colors, acrylic or watercolor, or anything else you choose. Once you are ready to begin, and have all the desired equipment, follow the steps below to create your own spiritual artwork.

STEPS TO CREATE A SPIRITUAL ARTWORK

1. Create a high frequency environment to allow Divine energies to connect with you more efficiently. (feng sui 9) Light a candle, put some soothing music on, pure in essential oils, even have crystals near me. This will help you to allow Divine inspiration more easily.

2. Similar to channeling, first you must invoke and allow Divine energies to guide you to a project. You do this with the following invocation:

> *"I lovingly call forth the most loving spirits, Angels or ascended masters, that can most assist me now, join me to create a beautiful spiritual artwork. Guide my movements, easily and efficiently until the artwork is completed. Thank you for your assistance, and so it is."*

3. Allow some time for the energy to gather with you; focus on your breathing and remove any thought. Take as much time as you need to you ensure that a spiritual connection has been established.

Inspiration strikes in various ways with different people. Some see each movement in their mind that indicates the color they should use, the brush, and the position of each line. Others might get a knowing as to what should be their next movement. In whatever way you receive instruction do not pause to think, just use it on the project. Spiritual artwork is guided step by step, for each movement you will receive new guidance.

4. Finish the entire project movement by movement. Once it is finished, there will be no more instructions. Admire whatever you have created and know that this may be a sign for you, an answer you have been seeking rather than simply a work of art. Thank Divine energies that guided you towards this project.

Spiritual artwork might help you find answers you have been seeking. Its benefits are similar to meditation, you enhance your spiritual connection, and you receive Divine energy within, as you learn to quiet your mind. Again, practice makes perfect. Every time you create a spiritual artwork, you get better at it.

52. HOW TO REMEMBER YOUR PAST LIVES

Before each reincarnation, physical beings undergo a temporary amnesia from past life times. This is to help them start new, not repeat the same mistakes, make new choices and experience new paths.

If you remembered who you were in the lifetime before, you would never fit in in the current life. You will want to continue what you left in the previous life. Nonetheless as we do no longer remember, we can start all over again, with fresh start and a clean slate. Even so, sometimes it benefits us to learn more about our past lives, it helps us to understand our current path, or see more clearly why we are on the current trail.

You might be a young or old soul; you might be wise as one or five thousand other lives. You might have incarnated only on earth, you might have visited other planes. You might have had good lives, while others might have been bad. The truth is most of us had experienced life both ways. This occurs in order to gain experiences and new traits. If for instance you were selfish and proud in one lifetime, in other you may choose to be depended on others to be more giving and appreciative. Yes, I did say "choose to be" because you decide who you want to be and what experiences to gain before each reincarnation. Nobody forced you to be in this physical body.

229

Remembering a past life is possible and many do it either to nourish their curiosity, practice their skills, or gain insight about who they are. Whatever is the way for you, I bring you the steps below.

Before you begin remember these vital first steps:

I. Protection (chapter 4)

II. Lie down in a comfortable position.

WAYS TO REMEMBER A PAST LIFE

1. One of the ways is through the **Akashic records**. See chapter 53. You can ask your guides and Akashic record keepers to take you through a past life.

> *"I ask for my guides to accompany me now in a past life regression journey. I ask the loving Akashic record keepers, and Archangel Metatron, to please <u>help me see an important event in any of my lives in order to help me understand this one. / help me be in an important even in my very previous life/ help me see a life that I was rich / help me see a life that I was someone famous...</u> (fill in your own words depending on what you want to achieve.)*
>
> *Have you noticed how the above invocation asks that they help you see? It is preferable to be able to "see" with your mind's eye what takes place. Whether you are clairvoyant or not, you will be able to experience a vision of a previous life. At the beginning you might only see a setting, other times you may be able to see people and even observe a conversation.*

2. Meditation. As you go into a deep meditation, create the intention to experience a past life. Ask your guides and the Akashic record keeps like the invocation above, to help you see it.

When you are relaxed enough, begin to climb a stairwell. At the end of the stairwell there is a door. You know that when you enter through the door you will be in a past life body.

While in a deep meditative state you will be able to see yourself in a past life, similar to seeing a dream. Set the timer beforehand to remind you to come back in the physical world.

There are also some very good guided meditations to help you experience a past life more easily.

3. **Hypnosis**. Of course I don't advise you do this on your own because you need someone to be present and help you come back whenever you need to. I suggest you find a professional of the field. They can direct you in a deep trance, and help you soul release in order to experience a past life.

I strongly suggest you record the whole session because you will not remember much after you wake up.

4. **Clairvoyance and intention.** Set your intention towards what you want to experience and know. Ask for protection and that your guides are present with you.

Close your eyes breathe slowly and the images will begin to form in your mind. You might get glimpses, flashes. You might be able to control what you see or just observe one setting.

If you are uncertain of where you are ask that proof is revealed for you. I usually ask to see myself in the mirror. Then I know who I am in that lifetime. You might even feel you know the surroundings, you might get certain emotions. Know that your guides are with you.

Whenever you are ready, ask to return back to your physical body. Allow some time to ground.

- *Usually you will be able to experience a past life regression in the first person. You will be able to see with your own eyes what takes place.*
- *You might see clear vision, you might only get glimpses, trust whatever you get. The more you practice the clearer the images will get.*
- *You will know whether what you see is indeed a past life, through the feeling. It will seem and feel familiar to you.*
- *Ground yourself when you are finished. (See chapter 7).*

53. HOW TO WORK WITH THE AKASHIC RECORDS

Akashic records are a spiritual plane that contains all decisions we ever took or would have taken, for all lifetimes, all lessons and experiences, thoughts and all interactions we ever had. Anything that we interact with in spirit or in physical form is recorded and exists through the Akashic records.

These records are very useful to spiritual beings that can study these records and recover memories, understand lessons or even relive a state of existence. The good news is that the Akashic records are exist so we can get a glimpse of them as well. Through them we can see our past lives and even future pathways.

In order to understand how the Akashic record work, let me give you an example. You want to move to a new house. As you think of possibilities, you create pathways. You think of moving to Atlanta, then you change your mind and you want to live in Kansas. The possibility of moving to Europe also crossed your mind. The Akashic records know your choices and create possible paths that lead to different outcomes.

We can enter the Akashic records and experience its teachings through our psychic abilities. Clairvoyant ability is preferred, but we can also experience the records through clairaudient ability. We can be anywhere we chose to as long as we allow it. There are times however, that we will not be unable to access them as it might intervene with our life teachings and free will.

Anyone has the right to enter the records no matter if you are advanced or a beginner. However, you can only observe and not interact.

When you are ready, begin with the following steps:

I. **Ask for protection**. Always ask to be protected so you don't get any interference.

II. Ask access to your Akashic records:

> *"I ask my spiritual team to help me connect with the Akashic records now. Loving record keepers grant me access now to find peace of mind, and answers to my questions. This is for the greatest and highest good. Thank you, and so it is."*

WAYS TO WORK WITH THE AKASHIC RECORDS:

1. **Automatic writing:** (reference chapter 40). You can ask and receive answers mentally. Write down the question, and the answer is going to be answered through your own thoughts.

2. Clairvoyance. This is the most fun way to enter in the Akashic records. Even if you are not highly clairvoyant, you can get glimpses and brief mental images.

Ask a question and then relax, clear your mind and the answers are going to come through mental images. I use this technique when I ask about the future or a past life. I see through the eyes of my future or past self and I can control what I see with ease.

3. Clairaudience. The record keepers or your guides will answer your questions according to what exists in the records.

Remember to have your questions ready beforehand, as well as a record player.

4. Pendulum dowsing. We have already gone through this technique and it is really easy. (Reference chapter 28.) You ask yes / no questions and see what comes up. You can also create charts with more answers and then follow the pendulum until it circles one. Let me give you a thorough example. You want to know a number, perhaps an age, or a year. Write numbers on a piece of paper and divide them. For instance write 20s on the left side of the paper, 30s on the middle and 40s on the right. You ask the pendulum to circle the age that you will be a parent. (Usually the years are already decided before you reincarnated so they already exist in the records). Guide the pendulum to the answers and it will automatically begin to circle one. Then you can continue on another paper by adding more specific years 31-33, 34-36, 37-19 and repeat. It is really easy and fun.

5. Crystal ball scrying. Similar to clairvoyance, the crystal ball is an instrument to help you receive the answer. You might see an image; you might even get a knowing for the answer. Trust it whatever it is. Reference chapter 47 on how to use a crystal ball.

6. **Meditation**. Even for this task meditation can be a very powerful ally. Set your intention before you begin so that your guides know what you want to achieve and they will guide you to receive your answer.

You can also try a guided meditation.

- The records cannot reveal any questions that intervene with another's free will.
- They will not allow you see something that you are not yet ready to.
- Ask only if you are ready to know the answer.
- Trust anything you receive.
- If you don't have success with any of the techniques, repeat when your mind is clearer.
- There is not one future path. If you see something from the future, it might only be a possible pathway.

54. PSYCHOMETRY – HOW TO SEE THE PAST IN OBJECTS

Anything that exists has energy. Non-living things capture the energy from their environment and from the people that hold them. Objects and clothes you own and wear hold part of your own energy. Anyone keen on psychometry, can read the energy of the person who has touched an object and the vibrations that it had stored. Psychometry is the ability to sense an object's history.

Objects get affected by high vibrations whether those are good or bad. If you wore one piece of jewelry for instance when you were crying, it will absorb low energy. When a psychometry practitioner touches it, it will sense sadness.

It is interesting to mention that since the objects you own absorb part of your energy, then those who have crossed over to the other side, still have a link with those items especially those that they favored in life. They can even try to communicate to the living through them.

Grandpa had a favorite rocking chair. He used to sit on it for hours, every time you saw him, he was on that chair. That chair has part of his energy. Grandpa knows that you associate that chair with him. if he wants to communicate, he will try to do so through that chair. When you sit on it, you might remember him strongly, get a weird sensation, smell him, or feel his love for you. You might even be able to see that chair rocking on its own. This could be a sign from grandpa saying hello.

The history of an object is created with energy. It is not overwritten when it changes hands, but records on its energy. Another example of object energy is through crystals. They can get "traumatized" by their handling or the way they were separated or cut from others of its kind. It then holds that negative energy within. This is why you need to cleanse all your crystals before you use them. Also, a house holds energy of all its owners. Likewise, a plant absorbs energy from its environment.

All you have to do is hold the item in your hand, set the intention of knowing its history. You might receive it through mental images, thoughts, emotions or knowing.

STEPS TO PHYCHOMETRY:

1. Choose an item, preferably an old one. It will be a good idea to borrow something from someone without knowing its history, just to see if you got something right afterwards.

2. Set your intention to receive the object's history as you hold it in your hands.

3. Clear your thoughts and experience what you receive. It might be an image, thought, an emotion or a knowing of what happened, or you might even see or sense its previous owners.

Take your time and don't stress yourself. If you don't get anything, try again another time, perhaps with a different object.

It's always a good idea to protect yourself first. (chapter 4)

55. HOW TO USE TELEKINISIS

Telekinesis is the ability to move objects with your mind. It requires concentration and the ability to focus on your thoughts. Everything exists in your mind already; you just have to learn to control it.

The idea behind telekinesis is that you use your own energy to move an object and not an external force.

STEPS TO TELEKINESIS

I. Believe it is possible.

II. Be determined to achieve it.

III. Find a very light object to practice at first. A good idea is to add a piece of paper or foil and place it on a pin in a way that is easy to move it.

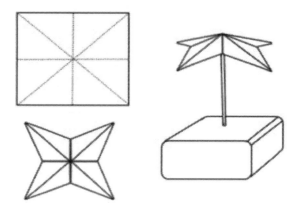

See picture:

You can try this with other light objects such as a feather. Trying to bend a candle's flame can also work.

At this point close any air-conditions or windows so the object does not move with the breeze. Otherwise, you can place the item in a glass jar.

IV. Release all thoughts.

V. Focus on the object as long as it is needed in order to feel it as an extension of you.

VI. Try any of the methods below.

1.

    a. Don't stand too close to the object.

    b. Visualize the change you want to do to the object whether it's bending it or moving it. In other words see the end result in your mind.

c: Have your eyes fixate on the object. Don't let anything distract you.

If it helps, slightly move your hands trying to imitate the movement you want to see like you are orchestrating it.

2. As you fixate on the object, image your Etheric arm moving towards the object and touching it.

3. Similar to chapter 16 on creating balls of energy, you can create energetic balls and then "throw" them or direct them towards the object in order to move it with their force.

- *Don't lose your focus. Even if the object moves, don't think, just observe. This way you don't lose your concentration, otherwise you will fail to move it.*

- *You can try to move it, make it go in circles, or even levitate. The energy and focus you use is just the same.*

- *Don't give up. The key is focus. If you train your mind to be released from thought you can succeed.*

- *You can move your hands according to the movement you the object to make. This is a good way to direct the energy in what direction to go.*

If you still don't believe telekinesis is possible, check out this guy:

https://www.youtube.com/watch?v=9dzYHuaFgp4

56. HOW TO DEVELOP YOUR TELEPATHIC ABILITIES

Telepathy, or mental communication, is the ability to communicate with someone through thoughts. This is the way spirits communicate with each other. Since we were all spirits, we have this ability within; all we need to do is practice it.

Telepathy transmits emotions otherwise known as clairsentience. It is the ability to feel and understand the emotions and feelings of people, animals, spirits, and places around you. You can also send thoughts, or images to another. You don't need to be close to another person to communicate telepathically, you don't even have to know them. Every one that has ever crossed your path, has created a link of connection with you, the so call "cord of connection". As a result when you think of a person, you call that cord in action. How many times did we think of someone and then we saw them the same day, or the phone rang with them on the other side? This is because you send them telepathic thoughts that they receive through the other side of that cord.

The messages don't always come through however. It depends on the other person's state of mind at that time. Perhaps you have successfully conveyed a message to them, but they were busy, they were sleeping, they were anxious, sad or occupied with other thoughts to receive it. Similar to a telephone, you might ring but that does not mean they will be available to pick up.

Everyone has used telepathy in one way or the other but follow the techniques below to use it intentionally.

WAYS TO DEVELOP YOUR TELEPATHIC ABILITIES

I. Believe. If you are a skeptic, the doors of your mind are closed and you will not be able to receive or sent any communication.

II. Be released from thought. It is always a good idea to meditate first, or use some breathing exercises to relax body and mind. This is true for both sender and receiver.

III. Get an image of a person you want to telepathically communicate with. You can also recall them clearly in your mind. Call their name three times. Release all thoughts and stare at their image either in front of you, or in your mind.

When you feel connected to that person, when you remember their essence, or many details about them such as smell, appearance, voice or/and posture you have created a vivid recollection of them and thus you have established a successful connection.

1. Visualization

a. Imagine that the person is a few feet away from you. See them, in detail. Feel them as if they are actually there.

b. Visualize a silver tube, or otherwise the cord of connection between you two, that connects your mind and theirs mind. This tube is full of energy.

c. Think of the thoughts or images you want to convey to the other person as clearly as possible. See them being transmitted through the tube and from your mind to their mind. Make the picture as vivid as possible. Add emotion to your thoughts and images as well so that they add more energy and force to be transmitted successfully

2. **Meditation**: While in deep meditation, visualize that you speak to the other person. Add as much detail as you can and hold the impression that this is in fact happening in real time.

3. Intention

a. Hold the intention of transferring your thoughts or images to them.

b. Think of what you want to say but make it really simple and distinct. You may want to say you are sorry, or ask that they phone you, or just show them an image of you, or even the image of a pineapple. Visualize the thoughts or images in your mind as clearly as possible.

c. Relax, knowing they have received the message.

IV. Know that the thoughts, images and emotions were successfully conveyed.

V. Cut the cords of connection. It is important to disconnect yourself from communication after you are finished. It is similar to a telephone call, when you are done, you have to hung up. If you don't disconnect, then you are going to keep transmitting thoughts, emotions to the other person or the opposite.

Don't worry cutting the cords of connection is a temporary process as a cord can be regenerated at any time you wish to communicate with them. See chapter 38 on how to.

VI. Check with the other person to find out if they have indeed received any images or thoughts resembling your own. The Receiver will be most receptive if they are relaxed and at ease. If successful, he or she will get several impressions coming through their mind such as emotions, colors, thoughts, images.

It is always a good idea to practice with another person who wishes to develop his/her telepathic abilities. In that case both of you meditate beforehand and try to send messages telepathically one at a time while checking regularly with each other.

57. HOW TO WORK WITH PLANTS

Plants are living, and as with anything that exist, they hold energy and vibration. You can train yourself to use the energy of plants as well as use your own to help them develop.

Recently an outstanding experiment was contacted that used words and their energy to see if they affect the plants. On the same two flower pots they wrote different labels "love" on the other "hate". They placed the plants under the same conditions and watered them similarly. The one with the word "love" grew and flourished, the other dried and died. In another similar experiment they placed two flower pots under similar conditions but they used high vibrational words to talk to the one, and low vibrational words to the other. The result was similar to the one above, the high vibrational words full of love and appreciation helped the plant grow and bloom, while the low vibrational spiteful words caused the plant to be destroyed. The experiments above show that plants get affected by the energy of their environment, and that includes people, words, thoughts and intentions.

I have already mentioned several times how valuable it is to be around trees and plants. They hold pure energies from earth they affect their environment. On the chapter on feng-sui for instance, (chapter 9). I have mentioned that placing healthy plants around your home and at your entrance welcomes good energy in your home. This is because the image and vibration of a healthy green or bloomed flower or tree is not only a great sight, but it showers its environment with healthy energy, purifies and rejuvenates its energy. This is very similar to the way plans create oxygen. They use the existent air and purify it with fresh oxygen. This goes without saying that the healthier the plant, the more oxygen and more energy it radiates. When you work with plants, you can recharge them with your own energy, help them grow and be healthy, while you can also use their healthy energy to purify your home.

WAYS TO ENHANCE THE HEALTHY ENERGY OF PLANTS

1. **Treat them with kindness and love.** Similar to the two experiments above, they need love to grow. Talk to them with kind words, tell them you love them, give them compliments. Be happy around them. As you project positive vibrations, you help your plants become healthy and vibrant. Who doesn't want to be treated with love?

2. **Intention**. As you plant a seed state in your mind or out loud that this plant will grow to be a healthy and beautiful one. This way you attract positive energy to work for both you and the plant. Know that this is going to be a great plant.

3. **Give it healing energy**. If you see a plant being unhealthy, visualize white healing energy surrounding it. Know that this energy will recharge and restore it.

4. **Bless the water**. Before you water your plants stand near your hose, or watering can and pray: "May this water be blessed and feed the plants so that they grow and be healthy"

5. **Invoke Angel or fairy assistance**. There are some Angels or spirits that work entirely with nature and they help to protect and nurture it. You can ask them to hang around your garden or house once in a while to make sure your plants turn out to be healthy and strong.

> *"I call forth loving spirits that work with nature and plants please take care of my plants so that they grow and become healthy and vibrant. Thank you thank you thank you for your kind assistance, much love and respect to you."*

6. **Connect with your plants telepathically.** As you may connect to any other object, you can use your clair abilities to talk to your plants. You can ask them what they need to be healthy. They can direct you whether they want more sun, more water, or simply more quiet. You can also ask them to purify the energy of your home, they love to help out.

7. **Place a crystal or gemstone near them**. If you place a healthy crystal under the tree or flower, it will charge and restore its energy. Remember to cleanse and program your crystal first.

58. HOW TO KNOW THE FUTURE

The future is not predestined. Psychics or even spirits cannot know the road your life will take. Your future has many pathways that are created as you walk along, as you make decisions, meet people, gain desires and create thoughts. Even though no one can know the end result, it is possible to tune into future possibilities.

Before you came in this physical reality, you have made a few choices about how this life will be. The choices include your current family, traits, and even your life's purpose or when you will have children. Perhaps you even knew some predestined possible pathways that you could be a president, or a janitor. The paths you ultimately choose however are based on your free will.

When the Angels or guides come forth to respond to a question, they always give some possible outcomes. In readings (visit: http://ameliabert.com/) people normally ask questions about the future. I give them possible pathways or even reveal the most likely event. You have to understand however, that according to your attention or else "the law of attraction" (see chapter 21) you direct the future. (For more details on this subject read: "The truth of all that is book")

All the possible future pathways, as well as existing ones exist in the Akashic records. When you access the records, you can ask for any information you desire past or present. For this some of the techniques I enlist below are similar to the ones you use to access the records.

Many people experience the future in different ways. If you are clairvoyant, you might get an image as a response to your answer, you might even be able to see yourself in a future setting. When you are in a future setting, you may not see things clearly but capture a general idea. For instance, when I asked to see my future home, I only saw a very general concept. I wasn't able to see furniture, colors or decoration. This is because those are decisions based on free will. Even the house I have seen, it was only a possibility. So overall, when you visit future pathways, don't expect to see the final outcome, or even many details. This is true only for future since past life paths have already been created.

You can also see, or access alternative future pathways. If you have decided to be a music teacher but you also wondered what it will be like performing professionally, then you can tune into the alternative pathway and see how things would have been. Seeing the future is fun but remember you can only observe.

WAYS TO KNOW THE FUTURE

1. Access the Akashic records of all knowledge. You can use any of the techniques in chapter 53 to enter the records. Remember what you receive will be the most possible pathway to an answer, or even capture multiple pathways.

2. Through Dreams.

a. Set the intention before you go to sleep. Decide what you wish to experience. You can even ask for something fun like "I want to see the future pathway of me being really wealthy in this lifetime."

b. Ask your guides to help you experience vivid dreams, as well as to remember them in the morning.

"I ask my loving guides, and the Akashic record keepers, please help me access my future and see clearly _____ in my dreams. Help me remember it when I wake up. Thank you, and so it is, for the highest and greatest good of all."

c. Believe that you will experience this future pathway in your dreams and go to sleep with that knowing.

d. Have a notebook ready and record your experiences as soon as you wake up.

3. *Intuition. This technique is really helpful for important decisions. In this method, you don't access the future pathways, but your guides and higher self do for you, and reveal the result through your intuition.*

a. Ask your question.

"I ask that I know as clearly as possible what will be the best decision for me right now regarding _____. I ask my guides, Angels and higher self please reveal it to me today. Help me know the right option that (<u>tell your guides what will make it a right choice for you. If it is a job is it more money, happy environment, gaining knowledge? Tell them so that they can direct you to it</u>.) Thank you, and so it is."

b. At this point you can only trust that you will receive the answer through your intuition. You will know without being able to explain why. Clear your head, and do not think about it again for the next two hours. At that time you can meditate, engage in a fun activity, sleep. By the end of the day you will have a clear understanding of the right decision, as a strong knowing.

There are times that we may not be able to receive answers or images to your questions about the future. This is because we must go through a learning process and find out some information ourselves.

When this happens, you will not receive a clear answer or image, but rather a more general one that may not answer your question or that it may not be what you were looking for.

Questions like seeing your future child, or your future husband, may not be granted. This is because the appearance of a child may not be chosen yet, or that there more than one possible future husbands for you.

59. BENEFITS AND DRAWBACKS OF BEING INTUITIVE

I have been on this amazing spiritual journey for two years now and I would not have it any other way. I have learned to appreciate all good and bad that comes with being an intuitive. Intuitive entails being an empath, a psychic, open to spirit, or having any of the Clair abilities. The more you open up spiritually, the more changes you will notice to you as a person, to your character, your attitude, but also to your own environment. Being on the spiritual path is a truly powerful way to live but as with anything, it needs a bit of getting used to.

The benefits of being intuitive are endless. You are in alignment with your passion, and with the universe. You bring a bit of both worlds in you; the spiritual and the physical. You recognize who you are where you come from and you make peace with yourself and the world. You are able to understand and answer many questions that were unanswered you couldn't before about you and the cosmos.

When you are spiritual, you take enjoy life, you are happier, more fulfilled, you follow your passions. You become stronger, wiser, joyful, peaceful, and confident; but most of all you believe in your own power. You want to help others, as you understand that we are all one. You recognize beauty all around; you learn to appreciate all that exists.

You unravel a bit more of your spiritual power each time you try and there so many new things to learn such Claraudience, clairvoyance, auras, telepathy, spirit communication, healing. As you learn to enhance spiritual connection your intuition enhances, you find yourself in the right places the right time, the universe has your back, and my most favorite, you achieve communication with spirit. You can work with your own spirit guides and Angels, to receive their wisdom, assistance, plus you have powerful allies and supporters at all times. This hidden power recharges you, only the thought of them makes you stronger.

Additionally, you are fulfilled because you understand that all exists within you and it is quite possible. You see the world in a new light, you understand that you are the cosmos and you value yourself more.

As you are in this new way of life, some things are no longer the same. This gift also has its shortcomings. As you are in a higher vibration, lower vibration experiences, tasks, or people are no longer a match with you. You might lose your job, your house, your life as you knew it, but most of all, your old friends. Of course this is not really a drawback as it is in fact a blessing in disguise. All of those lower vibration people or events only hold you back, so they need to be removed so new ones take their place. However, if you were surrounded with "friends", you suddenly find yourself being alone. People seem to move away, they don't want to see you again for no reason, they give up on you. Yes this might hurt of course, but you gradually realize that they were not real friends anyway. Eventually new, better ones take their place. The ones that support you, value you, understand and approve the real you.

You are more sensitive to the energies of others, and you can't stand being in a crowded room for long. You enjoy the quiet of your solidarity. If you enjoy meditation regularly, when you don't meditate for a few days you feel out of place. Also, you are keen to headaches and changes of vibration. Since you "fly high" in frequency when you are around people, events or experiences that don't fulfill you, you feel sick or drained.

You are more sensitive to your surroundings. If you are like me, when you are in a room with hundreds of precious stones you get nauseated, fatigued or breathless after a few minutes. Their strong energies of hundreds of gemstones or crystals might affect you and it will take two days to fully recover.

If you don't protect yourself regularly, certain spirits attach themselves to you and you feel drained. You are keen to headaches, ear buzzing, fatigues because now you are sensitive to your surroundings. Also, your hobbies change, even your taste in music; of course you embrace more beneficial and fulfilling ones tasks.

You might feel out of place sometimes. You get annoyed with close minded people and you are even forced to not be yourself around them to avoid contrast. That is especially true if your own family is not spiritual or open minded.

All in all, being intuitive or spiritual is a gift that needs to be treasured. I wanted to give you a word of caution as to what you might experience while on this amazing, inspiring journey. It becomes your new way of live, and believe me; you will not want to return to your old ways after that.

CERTIFICATE OF SPIRITUAL MASTERY:

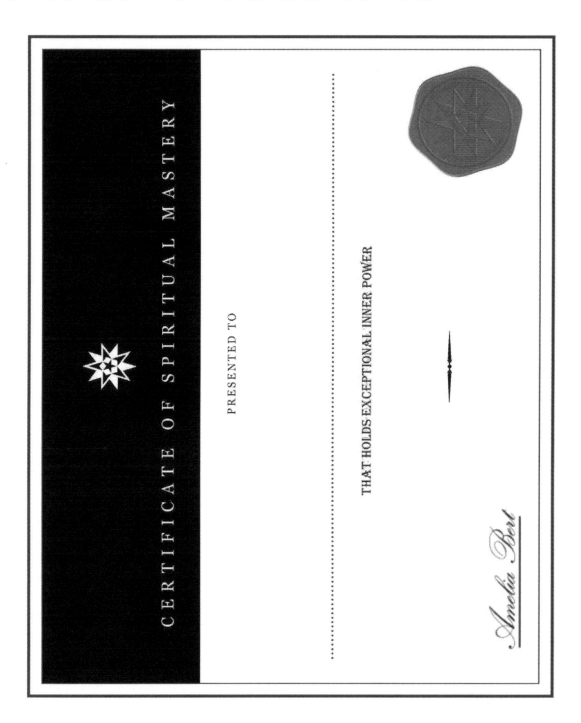

NOTE FROM THE AUTHOR:

Did you enjoy this book? If so, will you help the Angel's journey "Awaken" more people? Leave your amazing review on: http://www.amazon.com/

It would really matter to me.

As a spiritual teacher I collect recollections and experiences from spiritual practitioners to expand my expertise and put together in a future project. If you want to share your tips and experiences email me at: amelia@ameliabert.com

Sign up to my exclusive newsletter and get an instant 20% discount and gain access to free bonus materials, enlightening articles, and stay updated on future projects.

You can sign up here: http://ameliabert.com/

And follow me on social media:

https://www.facebook.com/theAngelbook/

https://twitter.com/Author_AmeliaB

https://www.linkedin.com/in/ameliabert

As a gift to you that you have made it his far, I give you a free EBook on Number Sequences, because even numbers bring you messages from spirit. *http://amzn.to/29kbVGt*

Many blessings to you.

OTHER WORKS FROM THIS AUTHOR:

THE TRUTH OF ALL THAT IS

In this book, the Angels respond to all your inquiries, thoughts and prayers. They share their wisdom, enlighten and empower. There are lessons to be learned, benefits to be gained, assistance to be given, truth to be revealed. They talk to you directly, if you would only allow the words to move through you, you will succeed your own personal transformation.

NUMBER SEQUENCES & THEIR MESSAGES

Do you get a glimpse of repetitive numbers? Do you notice number sequences like 1111, 222, 44 often?

They are not random, they bring you messages. They are Angel Numbers and in this booklet, you will learn all about them. Unravel them; discover their Divine Guidance.

INSIDE YOU WILL DISCOVER:

When numbers bring messages.   What do they mean; How to work with numbers to get answers to your questions.

GET THEM NOW IN ALL ONLINE BOOKSTORES! And from this website: http://ameliabert.com/

GET ANSWERS FROM THE ANGELS DIRECTLY

Do you want to connect with Amelia and the Angels to get direct assistance on your path, and answers to your questions?

Amelia is currently offering intuitive readings with your Guardian Angels and Spirit Guides. All you have to do is reach out.

We help you with an exclusive one time discount of 20% for any intuitive readings from the website:

http://bit.ly/1LGvTTT

Your answers are only a few clicks away.

OWN UNIQUE HIGH ENERGY ARTWORK

Hurry to get the original painting pieces of Amelia Bert. Those spiritual paintings were created with Angel inspiration and contain high energy that empower the space and people of their environment.

There are limited paintings, original and signed by Amelia Bert. Order and get your with free shipping worldwide!

http://bit.ly/1T7N3lz

ABOUT THE AUTHOR:

Amelia Bert is a freelance author and online journalist. At twenty five, she discovered her intuitive side, and mastered the clairaudient and clairvoyant ability to connect with spirit. She chooses to solely communicate with lighted spirits such as Angels that guide and inspire her.

She works closely with the Angels, through her psychic abilities. She gathers wisdom and information in that way, and shares it through her books and meditations. She aims to help others make a connection with their higher consciousness and discover their life's purpose.

Amelia has a degree in English language and literature. She spends her time writing, learning from the Angels, and painting. She lives with her fiancée and three cats and she plans to travel the world.

She wants to hear from you! Don't be shy, connect with her here: amelia@ameliabert.com

Made in the USA
San Bernardino, CA
29 May 2017